Fr. Bertrand W

His Cross in Your Life

CATHOLIC ANSWERS
SAN DIEGO
2000

Unless otherwise noted, Scripture quotations taken from the Revised Standard Version Catholic Edition (RSVCE) © 1946-1966, Division of Christian Education of the National Council of the Churches of Christ in the United States of America.

Reprinted with kind permission of the Congregation of the Passion, Fr. Terence Kristofak, C.P., Provincial

Published by Catholic Answers, Inc.
2020 Gillespie Way
El Cajon, California 92020
(888) 291-8000 (orders)
(619) 387-0042 (fax)
www.catholic.com (web)
Cover design by Laurie Miller
Printed in the United States of America
ISBN 1-888992-23-9

Contents

Preface

Fr. Bertrand Weaver was a Passionist priest, a prolific writer, and preacher, who died August 29, 1973. We lived in the same community in Union City, New Jersey, for some years before he died, and there one day we had a quick conversation I remember quite well, some thirty years later. He took a copy of the New York Times from under his arm and opened it to a story about a massive flood that claimed the lives of thousands of people in India the day before. "How can we explain the mystery of evil?" he asked with great feeling. "How can a good God permit something like this? I've asked myself this all my life."

Our conversation was quick because, inevitably, the mystery of evil leaves one at a loss for words, as it did us that day. But that incident of many years ago left me with an insight into Fr. Bertrand that stayed over time. His constant writing and preaching was his way of confronting a mystery, the mystery of evil, and the way he did it was not by human reason, but through another mystery, that of the cross.

His Cross in Your Life offers some thoughts that come from Fr. Bertrand's own long search into these twined mysteries. The cross of Jesus is not just the indispensable means of our redemption, it is also a powerful way to help us struggle with the mystery of evil in our lives and the questions it raises for us.

In this book, the author does not present the Passion of Jesus as a series of incidents based on what happened to him long ago. Rather, he begins with what happens to us, with the crosses we bear, and looks for wisdom and understanding in Jesus Christ. This is the secret of the saints who, throughout the centuries, have studied the lessons of the cross so diligently and well. They found in the cross the help they needed to make sense of their lives and the crosses they bore. Our age, too, stands in special need of the wisdom of the cross, as it faces the never-ending contradictions of human life.

"There is no surer sign that one is growing away from the mind and spirit of Christ than to grow away from the cross in one's philosophy of life," Fr. Bertrand writes. Conversely, the wisdom of the cross leads us to Christ, as a wise book from which we learn how to think about life, how to live, how to use this world, what to expect, what to hope for.

Fr. Victor Hoagland, C.P.
Saint Michael's Residence
Union City, New Jersey

Foreword

The meaning and message of the cross is so important that St. Paul resolved to know nothing among the Corinthians except Jesus Christ and him crucified. Pope John Paul II on one occasion declared that the celebration of the daily Eucharist was a way in which the Church herself responded to this admonition to know nothing except Jesus Christ and him crucified. When the secret of the saints is revealed, what we most often find is a profound union with Jesus Christ and him crucified: both an imitation of and a participation in the cross of Christ.

If we wish to live a serious Christian life, we, too, have to ponder the "secret" of the cross and learn how to imitate as well as participate in its power and profound love. We owe a debt of gratitude to Catholic Answers for bringing back into print Fr. Weaver's book on the cross.

Rather than a theoretical or abstract treatment of the theology of the cross, Fr. Weaver's focus is to show the links between the cross and our daily lives. Although written forty years ago, the wisdom of the cross displayed in this book remains ever relevant. Even when the examples used seem "dated," they add to the charm of the book, rather than detract from it, by their insight into the society of the time.

It is not possible to live in this life and not have suffering. As St. Catherine of Siena said, the issue is not whether to suffer or not to suffer, but whether to suffer with Christ or to suffer in isolation and loneliness. Those who seek to flee suffering simply find it in another form. Those who learn to embrace the cross and their suffering find a peace and joy that truly the world cannot give. This book helps us to find life, hope, and strength in suffering.

It is fitting that Fr. Weaver was a Passionist. A member of an order devoted to pondering and proclaiming the mystery of the cross, he fulfilled the charism of his congregation in an exemplary way. This is particularly meaningful for me, as it was outside the very monastery in Union City, New Jersey, where Fr. Weaver lived, after having visited one of the seminarians residing there, that God gratuitously gave me an understanding of the Father's love that has stayed with me to this day. And that love is nowhere more powerfully conveyed than in the cross of Christ.

Ralph Martin
Renewal Ministries
Ann Arbor, Michigan

Introduction

More than a century ago, John Henry Cardinal Newman wrote: "The great and awful doctrine of the cross of Christ may fitly be called . . . the heart of religion." For almost two thousand years, Christian writers have indeed looked upon the Passion and cross of the Son of God as the heart of the faith, the center and core of Catholicism. The Supreme Pontiffs and the Fathers and Doctors of the Church have given us a wealth of material to illuminate our thinking on the sacred Passion. Our understanding of the cross has been further enriched by preachers, poets, and artists.

The author of this volume hopes that he is not presumptuous in thinking that he offers a somewhat new approach to this most sacred subject. In what way is the approach new? It is new in stressing the fact that the Passion of our divine Redeemer appeals to the mind of man as well as to his heart. It is new in showing in detail how the cross throws light on every essential question that confronts mankind. It brings out what St. Paul had in mind when he wrote that Christ crucified is a manifestation of the "*wisdom* of God."

We have a tendency to forget that original sin not only weakened our wills, but also darkened our minds. We need, therefore, not only strength for our wills, but light for our intellects. This book emphasizes that from the cross streams the light we so greatly need.

It is the author's theory that much preaching produces only a passing effect because it appeals mainly to the emotions. It does not change people's thinking. As we think, so we act, and there is a great deal of wrong thinking. When we try to change a person's way of acting, we start by trying to change his way of thinking. This is why, in teaching Christian doctrine, we begin with what we call the dogmas of the faith—the Triune God, the Fall, the Incarnation, the Redemption, the Immortality of the Soul, etc. Only then do we go on to teach moral practice.

We have all seen those signs with the one word THINK. There is a business concern in this country that requests its executives to come to their offices a half hour early, and do nothing but sit at their desks and *think* for thirty minutes. The company involved realizes the direct connection between correct thought processes and correct action.

The author's aim is to get the reader to center his thinking around the cross. Anybody who does this is sure to see that the cross does answer every one of life's big questions, that it solves every one of life's main problems.

What are the great questions that concern mankind? Some of them are: *How long will I live? What is life's purpose? Why all this suffering? Can I achieve something worthwhile in life?* The cross answers these questions.

Consider other questions: *What is the right attitude toward the goods of this world? How do we fit prayer and penance into our lives? What is the most effective weapon against sin?* The cross also gives us the answers to these questions.

People ask: *How can we attain true peace of soul? What is the greatest proof of God's love for mankind? What is the best way to promote good human relations? How can we win eternal victory?* Again, the cross provides the answers.

Cardinal Newman might have been writing an introduction to this volume when he wrote in his great sermon, *The Cross of Christ, Measure of the World:* "His cross has put its value on all things which we see, upon all fortunes, all advantages, all ranks, all dignities, all pleasures; upon the lust of the flesh, the lust of the eyes, and the pride of life. It has set a price upon the excitements, the rivalries, the hopes, the fears, the desires, the efforts, the triumphs of mortal man. It has given a meaning to the various shifting course, the trials, the temptations, the suffering, of his earthly state. It has taught him how to use this world, what to expect, what to desire, what to hope. It is the tone into which all the strains of this world's music are ultimately to be resolved."

When the same peerless cardinal called the cross the heart of religion, he explained with unmatchable eloquence what he meant: "The heart may be considered as the seat of life: it is the principle of motion, heat, and activity; from it the blood goes to and fro to the extreme parts of the body. It sustains the man in his powers and faculties; it enables the brain to think; and when it is touched, man dies. And in like manner the sacred doctrine of Christ's Atoning Sacrifice is the vital principle on which the Christian lives, and without which Christianity is not."

1

Prologue

There is no symbol on earth on which the eyes of man rest more frequently than the cross. It is found on the tops of mountains and in wayside shrines. It rises from the domes and towers of cathedrals and basilicas, from the spires of churches and chapels in every part of the world. It is seen in the heart of the Christian world, where it crowns St. Peter's Basilica, and in the heart of the Red empire, where it still looks down, inexplicably, from St. Basil's Cathedral.

This exaltation of the cross is a supplementary mark of the true Church. The Church will not allow anybody, if she can help it, to escape the sight of the cross. But the Church does not want men merely to see it physically. She wants them to see and understand it mentally and spiritually. St. Matthew states that, after the executioners had nailed the Son of God to the cross, "they sat down and kept watch over him there" (Matt. 27:36). These men, indeed, saw the cross, but they saw it as nothing more than an instrument of execution. They did not understand that what they had used as a gibbet our Lord was using as a pulpit.

The Church exalts the cross because it is the means by which divine wisdom willed to save mankind. She exalts it also because her divine Master taught from the cross a complete philosophy of life. Philosophy means the love of wisdom. And wisdom is a knowledge of what is true and right. Christ on the cross demonstrates what is true and right for man in his present fallen state. From the cross, God himself is telling man how to think and act wisely in this passing world.

It is certain that man can reject the wisdom of the cross only to his eternal peril. It is evident, moreover, that his earthly happiness also depends upon his accepting it. In middle Europe, millions rallied around a cross which, as Pius XI said, was not the cross of Christ. They hailed as a new book of wisdom the Mein Kampf of a man who, in his towering folly, was to pull much of Europe down in ruins around him. The world has seen the exaltation of the supposedly wise writings of the false prophets of Communism, and it has witnessed the incredible misery which these writings have brought upon mankind.

In humiliation, mankind saw so-called Christian statesmen at Yalta, Potsdam, and other gatherings of the world's reputedly wise men turn their backs on the wisdom of the cross and manifest such folly that generations will have to pay the price of it. To such apply the words of Isaiah, which St. Paul repeated when writing of the wisdom of the cross: "I will destroy the wisdom of the wise, and the cleverness of the clever I will thwart" (1 Cor. 1:19). St. Paul goes on to state that man no longer has a choice among schools of wisdom. Since God came into his world to teach man wisdom, particularly through the cross, man either accepts this wisdom or he perishes.

St. Paul makes this clear when he says: "For since, in the wisdom of God, the world did not know God through wisdom, it pleased God through the folly of what we preach to save those who believe. . . . But we preach Christ crucified, a stumbling block to Jews and folly to Gentiles, but to those who are called, both Jews and Greeks, Christ the power of God and the wisdom of God" (1 Cor. 1:21–24). St. Paul is echoing our Lord's reply to Peter when the latter chided Christ after he had foretold his intention of giving himself up to the cross: "Get behind me, Satan! . . . For you are not on the side of God, but of men" (Matt. 16:23).

There is no surer sign that one is growing away from the mind and spirit of Christ than to grow away from the cross in one's philosophy of life. Conversely, it is overwhelmingly evident that the closer one draws to the mind and spirit of Christ, the more one's thought and action are shot through with the wisdom of Calvary.

When one considers the matter deeply enough, one comes to the conclusion that the saints are the only completely wise members of the human race. And one characteristic common to the saints is their absorption in the cross, their application of its teaching to their own lives, and their blazing zeal in helping others to see and act on its wisdom. The crucifix used in so many representations of the saints is no mere prop. Whether it is a St. Thérèse holding it in her hands as she is wrapped in contemplation of its wisdom, a St. Paul of the Cross pointing to it in a preaching gesture, or a St. Francis Xavier holding it aloft as a beacon to the infidel, it is clear that such various representations are only one way of saying that the thought and action of the saints revolved around the cross.

One can judge men's thoughts by their speech. And the saints speak as one when it comes to the cross. The cross, for them, is the center of revelation, the pivot about which all Christian mysteries revolve, the encyclopedia of divine wisdom, the answer to every question, and the solution to every problem, personal or universal.

Whether the statement comes from one of the most profound thinkers of the ages, such as St. Augustine, or from a humble friar, such as St. Francis, if it is a statement about the cross, there is a remarkable similarity. St. Augustine revealed the source of his wisdom by saying that "there is *nothing* so salutary for us as to think every day of what Jesus, who is God and man, has endured for our sakes." And St. Francis, whose wisdom has charmed the whole world and caused hundreds of thousands of Franciscans proudly to bear his name, uncovered the wellspring of his wise way of life by saying to his friars: "My brethren, constantly keep before your minds the way of the cross upon which our Lord Jesus has led us; the more one conforms oneself to Jesus crucified, the more one will become like to God."

Albert Einstein, who was a great mathematician but hardly noted for his overall wisdom, left his brain to science, thinking that the secret of his mathematical genius might be discovered in the convolutions of this mass of matter. A careful analysis revealed nothing that notably differentiated his brain from any other. A genius of a far different order, St. Thomas Aquinas, whose philosophical and spiritual wisdom still awes mankind after seven centuries, did not have to wonder about the source of his wisdom. He revealed the secret of it to the world when he said that he gained more wisdom through prayer at the feet of the crucified than from all the books he had ever read.

Two founders of modern religious congregations, established especially to preach the wisdom of the cross, also left no doubt where their thought and action derived its inspiration. St. Paul of the Cross, founder of the Passionists, declared: "I would believe myself to have failed in duty if I were to pass a single day without thinking of my Savior's Passion." And St. Alphonsus, founder of the Redemptorists, whose wisdom was crowned with the title of Doctor of the Church, stated that "*nothing* is more wholesome than to make the cross the subject of our thought at least once a day."

Professed agnostics frequently pay tribute to the wisdom of Jesus as it shines resplendent from the pages of the Gospels. One of Britain's outstanding journalists, Malcolm Muggeridge, for example, has observed, in connection with space rockets, that no human discovery or invention could affect the profundity of the Sermon on the Mount. What the skeptics, and even some Christians, fail to see is that all the wisdom of the Mount of the Beatitudes was underscored on the Mount of the Crucifixion. All the divine wisdom taught by word on the first mount was taught by demonstration on the second.

That many lives are untouched by the wisdom emanating from these hallowed hills is mankind's great tragedy. Almost two thousand years after this wisdom was given to the human race, there is still too much truth in the saying, "What fools these mortals be!" Those who have been entrusted with the wisdom of the cross, the wisdom of God, can take no complacency in the spectacle of men making fools of themselves. And we who are Christians but not saints must humbly admit that we are partly responsible. Too often we fail our fellowman because we do not study and apply the wisdom that we claim to exalt.

Because the Sermon on the Mount of Calvary was preached in a divine silence, only those who are willing to listen in this kind of silence can hear its message. It is only by plunging into the silence of religious thought and prayer that one can hear the divine voice of the crucified.

There is in the cross a mine of wisdom, more precious than all the gold, diamonds, or uranium in the world. But mining involves work. If men are willing to make prodigious efforts to uncover the wealth hidden in the earth, how can the followers of the Master be idle when Calvary is waiting to yield the riches of divine wisdom? The saints have set an example of prospecting for and mining this wisdom. Anybody can share in their eternal riches if he is willing to share in their efforts.

2

His Cross And Life's Purpose

It is only natural to look for formulas that will help to simplify our lives in this complex world. The desire for formulas is so universal that a book with such a title as Happiness through Respiration, Happiness through Dieting, or Happiness through Willpower would have a pretty good chance of making the bestseller lists. It should be obvious by now that books offering formulas for successful or happy living do not have to be based on valid psychological principles or authentic religious concepts to gain wide circulation.

This is not to say that there is anything wrong with formulas for successful living. Nobody, however, can offer a valid formula unless he knows the purpose of life. And Christ made it as clear as the light from an atomic explosion that the whole and only purpose of our life on earth is not to rise to the top of the social ladder, nor to amass material goods, nor to escape pain and tension for 365 days a year, but to do God's will.

That the one, great, overall purpose of life is the accomplishment of God's will runs like a golden thread through both the Old and New Testaments. In the Old Testament, we see the dramatic way in which God tested Abraham to prove whether or not the patriarch's will was attuned to his own. And who can forget the way God tried Job? David also was tested and stood up so well that God declared him to be "a man after my own heart, who will do all that I desire." The Redeemer's mission was summed up concisely in the Old Testament psalm in which David placed on the lips of Christ the words: "In the head of the book it is written of me that I should do thy will: O my God, I have desired it, and thy law is in the midst of my heart."

When our Lord had come, he said simply: "I have come down from heaven, not to do my own will, but the will of him who sent me." He told his disciples that he subsisted on the will of his Father: "My food is to do the will of him who sent me." He gave as a proof of the authenticity of his doctrine the fact that he fulfilled his Father's will: "And my judgment is true because I seek not my own will, but the will of him who sent me."

He left no doubt that the performance of his Father's will would be the supreme criterion by which men would be judged on the day of reckoning: "Not everyone who says to me, Lord, Lord, shall enter the kingdom of heaven; but he who does the will of my Father in heaven shall enter the kingdom of heaven." In the Our Father, he taught us to pray: "Thy will be done on earth as it is in heaven."

In view of all this, an authentic formula for successful and happy living can be proposed. The formula is: *The only thing that should concern us, twenty-four hours a day, 365 days a year, is the present, evident will of God.* This formula would be more widely accepted if the present, evident will of God did not sometimes involve crucifixion. Nobody would ever object to doing God's will if it always brought the sense of exultation reflected in the line of the well-known song: "God made thee mine!"

It is when God's will means physical pain or mental anguish that man needs the cross—that aspect of Christianity which many people seem to believe will go away if they ignore it. A crossless Christianity is a heretical fraud. Those who attempt to offer Christ without his cross are cheating humanity. They are leaving those who accept their spiritual nostrums without sufficient defense against the tragedies which are woven into every human life.

Those who avert people's gaze from the holy Tree which God caused to be erected at the crossroads of the world and from which the Son of God preached the only wisdom that can save mankind are robbing others of their divine heritage. They are prompting them to escape from, or to waste, what Christ has shown through his cross to be one of the most precious things in human life— suffering accepted as part of God's mysterious design.

Since the fall of man, God has always asked human beings to accept or to undertake what is difficult or painful. But the most difficult, painful, and heroic sacrifice that God ever asked was that which he asked of his own Son.

Because so many crucifixes completely fail to convey a sense of the world's central tragedy, people have little understanding of the appalling reality of Calvary. The world is filled with crucifixes of gold, marble, and wood, and of those made from less desirable materials. Most of them accomplish little in helping the viewer to visualize the living Christ stretched out in the most savage and brutal form of execution ever devised by inhuman minds.

An idea of the fearful implications of the Crucifixion can be gained indirectly when one considers how the Savior shrank from the ordeal of Calvary with horror and dismay when he envisioned it in Gethsemane. Courageous as he had been in driving the moneychangers from the Temple, heroic as he had shown himself in condemning evil and revengeful men in positions of power, the realization of the torture, humiliation, and abandonment of the cross caused him to sweat blood.

Isaiah said that Christ offered himself in this tremendous act of sacrifice because he willed to do so. But he forced his human will to accept that from which his humanity recoiled. When, on the cross, he was drinking to its bitter dregs the chalice of wormwood and gall that had so revolted his human nature in the garden, he was draining it because it was his Father's will. He was saying to the last dread gasp: "Not my will, but thine be done."

Love is a union of wills. And the love of God is a union of man's will with God's. It is so easy to unite one's will with God's when what he wills is sweet and easy, when his will fits hand in glove with one's natural inclinations. But if all our days were filled with completely satisfied natural desires—ideal living conditions, economic success, robust health—how could we ever know that it was God's will, and not our own, that we were seeking?

It is only when his will is opposed to what we would naturally choose, only when his will takes the form of a cross, and it is still embraced, that we can be sure that it is not our will, but God's, that we want to see exalted.

If the whole purpose of life is to do the will of God, and if the only sure test of acceptance of his will is acceptance of the cross, the cross should actually be received joyfully. If the cross is lacking from his life, a person should begin to wonder whether God considers him worth testing. St. Paul expresses one of the great paradoxes of Christianity when he says that what is to be feared is not the cross, but the absence of it. He could not have expressed this idea more vigorously: "But if you are without chastisement, whereof all are made partakers, then you are bastards, and not sons." It was this idea which inspired John Donne to write: "No cross is so extreme as to have none."

The only thing feared by those who truly seek God is that their lives will not be sufficiently signed with the cross. Realizing that acceptance of trial, as the very word *trial* indicates, is the one conclusive way they have of knowing whether they have sacrificed their own wills and are seeking the will of God, their ambition is to be able to say with St. Paul: "With Christ I am nailed to the cross." St. Thérèse was expressing a conviction that should be part of the thinking of every member of the Church when she said: "What I fear is not suffering, but my own will."

Incidentally, it is a waste of time to wonder whether one fulfilled God's will last year, or ten or twenty years ago. If we failed in doing his will in the past, it is sufficient that we have a general contrition for all past failures. It is a mistake to fret over them in detail. If God not only forgives but forgets sincerely repented mistakes, why should one go back and pick over them?

It is also not helpful to wonder what God's will may be for us next week or next year. Christ said: "Do not be anxious about tomorrow, for tomorrow will have anxieties of its own. Sufficient for the day is its own trouble." Cardinal Newman observed, in connection with possible future trials, that one should not wonder how one would measure up in a time of persecution. He said that extraordinary graces would be given which are needed at such a time. This is true of any future trial.

It is important to concentrate, therefore, on the *present* will of God. After all, there is only the present day, the present hour. The past is gone forever and nobody knows the length of his future, nor what it will bring. God's will in the present hour is always clear. He makes his will completely *evident* through his Commandments, one's state in life, and the circumstances and events of which life is woven.

Some of life's circumstances and events are joyful. Other events and circumstances are sorrowful. God wills both. The difficulty is the attitude that should be maintained when his present, evident will involves the acceptance of the cross.

When a cross is presented in the form of sickness, temptation, family trouble, financial difficulty, or whatever shape it takes, it is certainly not contrary to the will of God that one ask to be delivered from it. Our Savior himself prayed in Gethsemane: "Father, if it be possible, let this chalice pass from me." But when it is seen, as in the case of Christ, that the Father's will is that one accept the cross proffered, one must finish one's prayer as Christ did: "If this chalice may not pass away, but I must drink it, not my will, but thine be done."

St. Gabriel, the Passionist scholastic, and St. Thérèse, the Carmelite contemplative, suffered dreadfully from the consumption which took their lives when they were twenty-four years of age. There is no record that they prayed to be cured. Perhaps they did. Whether they did or not, they realized that God was asking them to unite their cross with the cross of Christ. This was God's *present, evident* will for them. Thus they achieved the perfection of that heroic sanctity which has raised them to the altars of the Church. By becoming one with the Christ of the Crucifixion, they have become one with the Christ of the Resurrection. In them, and in all like them, there is a wonderful fulfillment of the words of St. John: "And the world passes away, and the lust of it; but he who does the will of God abides forever" (1 John 2:17).

3

His Cross And The Heart Of God

Nothing is more important in the living of the Christian religion than understanding God's purpose in strewing our path to eternity with crosses. His purpose becomes clearer in proportion to our understanding of St. John's teaching that God is love. Once we realize that God loves us with a love whose fullness we will comprehend only in eternity, we realize that anything which God wills for us must be good for us, appearances to the contrary notwithstanding.

If it had not been for divine revelation, men might have gone on forever arguing about God's attitude toward mankind. On the one side would have been those who held that ferocious beasts, poisonous reptiles, death-dealing cyclones, fire, and pestilence proved God's indifference to his creation. On the other side would have been those who claimed that the miracle of beauty called spring, the majesty of an elm, the loveliness of a rose, the smile of a baby, the perfection of a human body, and the unwavering goodness of a saint demonstrated that the Creator was a God of love.

For the person of faith, the matter is decided. Revelation shows the Creator as a God of boundless love. The very fact of revelation is proof of his love. In the Old Testament, there are endless evidences of God's loving interest and care. Noah, Abraham, Moses, and David could all testify to the love and goodness of God. The books of Tobit, Judith, Esther, and Job bear out the testimony of the psalmist: "How good God is to the upright; the Lord, to those who are pure of heart!"

Even the prophets, who thundered against sin and spoke so much of divine retribution, give us the most moving testimonials of the Almighty's love. "He shall feed his flock like a shepherd," says Isaiah, "he shall gather together the lambs with his arm, and shall take them up in his bosom." In another place, the same prophet says: "In his love and mercy he redeemed them, and he carried them and lifted them up all the days of old."

"Yea, I have loved thee with an everlasting love," says God through Jeremiah. Jeremiah also chiefly echoes the appealing refrain: "I will be their God, and they shall be my people."

But it was not until the world had been prepared for God's full revelation that "the goodness and kindness of God our Savior appeared." And then the love of God revealed itself in such a surging tide of mercy, love, and self-giving that human language cannot begin to describe it. Men speak glibly about God's becoming man, about the divine wisdom that poured from his lips, about his going up and down Palestine seeking the lost sheep of the house of Israel, and often one wonders if a reverent silence would not be more fitting in the face of such a love as that of the Heart of God.

The words of St. Augustine regarding the gift of the Eucharist are profound and eloquent: "I dare say that God, in his omnipotence, could not give more; in his wisdom, he knew not how to give more; in his riches, he had not more to give." But there is always the feeling that even the greatest human expression falls short when lauding the love for which all subsequent love is named.

If one stammers and stutters in the face of the mystery of God's love in general, one must feel completely tongue-tied before the manifestation of that love through the cross. There is eloquence in the simple statement of St. John: "In this we have come to know his love, that he laid down his life for us." Human protestations of love can be deeply moving. Divine protestations of love are baffling and overwhelming. "But God *commends* his love toward us," writes St. Paul, "because when as yet we were sinners, Christ died for us."

The divine Redeemer appeals to his offering of his life as the supreme proof of love: "I am the Good Shepherd. The Good Shepherd lays down his life for his sheep." At the Last Supper, in commanding his Apostles to imitate his love, he said: "Greater love than this no one has, that one lay down his life for his friends." God's love for man is infinite. Such a love must choose the ultimate way of proving itself. The final proof of love is to give one's life for the one loved.

G. K. Chesterton, with the fresh insight which he brought to the truths of the faith, drew the logical conclusion that, if Poverty could be called the bride of St. Francis, there was no impropriety in speaking of Death as the bride of Christ. He brings this out in a comparison between the death of Socrates and the death of Christ: "We are meant to feel that the death of Socrates was, from the viewpoint of his friends at least, a stupid muddle and miscarriage of justice interfering with the flow of a humane and lucid philosophy. We are meant to feel that Death is the bride of Christ, as Poverty was the bride of St. Francis. We are meant to feel that his life was in that sense a love affair with death, a romance of the pursuit of the ultimate sacrifice."

Death, like poverty, is a negation. Poverty is the result of being stripped of physical goods, and death is the result of being stripped of physical life. Nobody criticizes St. Francis for speaking romantically of *Lady* Poverty. If there can be spiritual romance in the pursuit of Poverty, there can be far more romance in the pursuit of Death. This whole way of talking has to be kept in its proper frame of reference, namely, sacrifice. Neither poverty, nor death, can be sought for its own sake. To seek negation for its own sake is irrational.

Christ said that he was anxiously awaiting his death. But he was looking forward to it as the great opportunity to demonstrate his love for mankind. His attitude toward death was a positive attitude—a romance of the pursuit of the ultimate sacrifice.

When the God of love willed to give the final proof of his love, "being found in human form he humbled himself and became obedient unto death, even death on a cross" (Phil. 2:8). Even what would have been regarded as the ultimate sacrifice, the simple giving of one's life, was not enough of a manifestation of the infinite love of God. Thus he would not only offer his life, but offer it in a manner so incredible that only miracles, preceding and following, have made it credible. For the Son of God poured out his life's blood through hands, and feet, and side. And this on a cross, most savage of all instruments of execution.

There are those who would accept this sublime idea of a God sacrificing his life on a cross if it were served up as a Greek tragedy, without the challenge to the human heart that is involved if one takes the story literally. When George Santayana said that Christianity is true poetically, he apparently was saying that it is too good to be true that God should have become man, and especially that he should have shed his blood for us. This would be to say that God could not love to the point of ultimate sacrifice.

This extreme of giving does appear perhaps to be too much of a good thing. Many are ready to join Peter in remonstrating with Christ: "This will never happen to thee." But Peter was to become so convinced of the attractiveness of the romance of the pursuit of the ultimate sacrifice, that he eagerly reached out to share through his own crucifixion. The bewildering love demonstrated by the Crucifixion of the Son of God has continued to overwhelm Christian mystics. But if there have been remonstrances on the part of the mystics, they have been figurative, like Richard Crashaw's:

> Thee with Thyself they have too richly clad,
> Opening the purple wardrobe of Thy side.
> O never could there garment be too good
> For Thee to wear, but this of Thine own blood.

St. John would have had to have been one of the great poetic geniuses of all time to have *created* the dramatic climax of the story of God's love for man, the thrusting of the lance into his side, plunging through until it pierced the Heart, the Heart of God. The Evangelists omitted many details of the Crucifixion, but the lance's thrust is underscored because the blood and water that gushed forth symbolize the fullness of his giving. The Sacred Heart is now shown with the wound made by the lance, because the soldier's thrust not only opened his side, but his Heart. As Pope Pius XII wrote: "The lance's thrust certainly reached the Heart, inasmuch as the soldier's purpose in wielding it was to make certain beyond all doubt that Jesus Christ crucified was dead."

Gods love is the source of all his external action. For this reason, all the graces received by the Church, and the very Church herself, have been regarded as springing from the pierced side of the Savior. An inscription on the Lateran Baptistery reads: "The font of life which spills over the whole world flows from the wounded side of Christ."

It is hardly surprising, in view of all this, that Pope Pius XII wrote, "The Heart of Christ is the clearest image of the fullness of God embracing all things. By this we mean the fullness of mercy, which is the special characteristic of the New Testament." Nor is one surprised any longer by the statement of Pope Leo XIII, which at first appears startling: "Devotion to [the Sacred Heart] is the most excellent form of religion."

In the face of such love, one perhaps can be content to let the Byzantine hymn attempt to express the inexpressible:

> No hymn that seeks to weave into one
> Thy many mercies is worthy of Thee:
> were we to bring Thee, O holy King,
> odes many as the sea sand we should
> do nothing worthy of what Thou
> has given us who sing to Thee.

4

His Cross And Prayer

When man recognizes the indescribable love that God has for him, he reaches out to embrace God. He experiences a great desire to commune with the One who loves him so much. God encourages this communion by encouraging man to pray. The closer one approaches God, the more frequent and spontaneous is one's conversation with him in prayer.

How spontaneous and effective such communing with God can become is illustrated by those who have drawn closest to him, the saints. A concrete example is found in the story of the teenage French girl who one time was eagerly searching through the daily paper for the story of a three-time murderer. Some years later she wrote: "On the day following the execution, I hastily opened the paper, *La Croix*, and looked for the part concerning Pranzini. Without confession or absolution, Pranzini mounted the scaffold, and the executioners were dragging him toward the fatal block when all at once, apparently in answer to a sudden impulse, he turned around, seized a crucifix which the priest held toward him, and kissed our Lord's sacred wounds three times!"

The reporter who wrote the story for *La Croix* obviously recognized this as a sensational conversion, especially since it was public knowledge that the notorious criminal had decided to die unrepentant. But this now nameless reporter missed a scoop. The girl who was avidly reading the paper the next day could have given him some eternally interesting background material, although likely neither he nor his editor would have believed it.

Thirty-odd years later this girl was to make the newspaper herself through her triumphant canonization as St. Thérèse of Lisieux. She rounded out the Pranzini story in her autobiography by telling how she had overheard her elders talking about the condemned man's impenitence. She simply asked God for Pranzini's soul, adding that she was completely certain her prayer would be heard, but begged for "just one sign of repentance" because this was her "first sinner."

No reader of *La Croix* that day would have surmised that an obscure fourteen-year-old girl in the town of Lisieux had been responsible for the dramatic climax to the story of Pranzini's execution. Being to such an extent creatures of sense, men give a great deal of attention to things they see and hear, while the vast world of the unseen receives little or no notice. Prayer like that of the young Thérèse is constantly rising from hundreds of thousands of human hearts. People take as much notice of this phenomenon as they do of the invisible electrical impulses that fill the air all around them and bring sound or image to their radios or television sets.

The sacrificial prayer of Christ on the cross went unnoticed by most of those standing on Calvary. Once when he prayed in the midst of his agony, using the words of a psalm which should have been familiar to many of those gathered about the cross, they thought, or pretended to think, that he was invoking Elijah.

The prayer of our Savior in Gethsemane has been fruitful as a source of inspiration throughout the Church's existence. Not enough attention is given, perhaps, to the prayer of Christ on the cross. The Gospels make various references to the efficacious prayer of the Son of God made man. He was always heard "because of his reverent submission," but the sacrificial prayer of his sacred Passion had an even more wonderful efficacy. That sacrificial prayer, begun under the olive trees in the garden, reached its climax on the cross.

Only seven brief utterances of the crucified Redeemer have been recorded. Four of these seven utterances were prayers. At least two of these four were verses from the psalms, and Christ was probably praying in the words of the psalms even when not speaking these words aloud. One gets the impression that, except for several interruptions when he spoke to our Lady, St. John, and the Good Thief, Christ spent all the time on the cross praying to his eternal Father.

Through his communing with his Father, he created such an atmosphere of prayer around the cross that such unlikely subjects as the Good Thief and the centurion were caught up in it. Only the power and example of the divine Master's prayer could have moved the hardened criminal hanging next to him to pray, although praying was probably the last thing he expected to do when preparations were being made for his crucifixion.

Jesus had prayed at every juncture in his earthly life. Before starting his public ministry, he had prayed in the desert for forty days and nights. He prayed all night before choosing his Apostles. As his Passion was about to begin, he went to the Mount of Olives to pour out his soul in fervent prayer. And now that his Passion is reaching its climax on the cross, his prayer is also reaching its height in fervor and power.

Again Christ is using the cross as a pulpit. He is telling man through his prayer on Calvary that if he is wise, the first thing he will do in time of crisis, in time of stress, difficulty, or temptation, is to pray. Instead of turning to God by a sort of divine instinct at such times, many people wring their hands in utter futility or seek comfort and support in creatures. They act as though God knew nothing about their plight, when the truth is that he has offered them the cross for the precise purpose of bringing them closer to him.

One of the great disadvantages of failing to pray in times of trial is that the failure to pray involves the most tragic of all wastes—the waste of our crosses. One of the three crosses on Calvary was wasted because the second thief, instead of imitating his companion by prayerful acceptance of his trial, rebelled and blasphemed. The Good Thief shows that one of the most salutary effects of immediate prayer in time of trial is that it causes one spontaneously to offer God the thing which is so difficult to solve or to bear.

By prayerfully offering to God whatever is difficult, one attains the main purpose of prayer, which is to unite our wills with God's will. This was the chief effect of the Savior's prayer during his Passion. Never in the history of the world had it been so difficult to accept the will of God. St. Paul, who never tired of writing about Christ's obedience to his Father's will, shows our Lord's conformity to the will of his Father reaching its height when he says that Christ was made obedient unto death, even to death on a cross.

On the cross, the Master emphasized the interaction that exists between prayer and obedience to God's will. He prayed in his Passion to do his Father's will. As a result, he fulfilled that will perfectly. And because of this complete conformity, his prayer became completely efficacious. St. Paul says that it was this prayer, backed by his perfect obedience, that obtained his Resurrection. "Jesus, in the days of his earthly life," writes St. Paul, "with a loud cry and tears, offered up prayers and supplications to him who was able to save him from death, and was heard because of his reverent submission. And he, Son though he was, learned obedience from the things he suffered."

Christ teaches mankind especially from the cross that man's prayer is the outcome of his understanding and acceptance of his teaching and spirit. If we have his spirit, our prayer will be like his. There will be the same interaction referred to above. We will pray, in the first place, to do God's will. He will keep his promise and give us the grace to do it. And, doing his will, our prayer will become progressively more efficacious.

If a person has the spirit of Christ, which is essentially a spirit of obedience, his prayer will never degenerate into an effort to bend God's will to his. He will never offer his petitions in the spirit of a strike-it-rich program. Woven into every prayer offered will be the all-embracing petition of the Lord's Prayer, *thy will be done on earth as it is in heaven.*

It is not unusual to hear people complain that their prayers are not answered. This complaint appears to come mainly from those whose only prayer seems to be that of petition for temporal favors. One factor in many unanswered prayers is obviously the failure of those praying to carry out the will of God, especially when his will is difficult. Only if one is doing God's will as manifested in his Commandments, and accepting his will as revealed through the events of life, can one claim to be identified with the crucified Savior. And only when one has become identified with Christ does one deserve to be heard by the eternal Father.

When the purpose of our prayer becomes the same as the purpose of our Lord's prayer on the cross, namely, a union of our wills with God's, our prayer does not simply become *like* the prayer of Christ. It becomes *one* with his. Since, through membership in his Mystical Body, all share in the priesthood of Christ, our prayer *must* become one with his if it is to be truly efficacious.

St. Thérèse, by establishing a one-saint siege before the Throne of Grace, obtained the last-minute repentance of a notorious criminal. An important aspect of the story is this: Realizing that of herself she could do nothing to obtain this tremendous grace, she asked it through the infinite merits of the Redeemer. She understood the power of prayer. And, young theologian that she was, she saw that prayer which is not offered with and through Christ is offered in a vacuum.

When we are praying in the spirit of Christ, when our prayer becomes one with his, we are truly praying in his name. And when this happens, we understand and experience the full impact of those beautiful and powerful words of the sacred liturgy: "Through Jesus Christ, your Son, our Lord." Repetition is often tiresome, but the repetition of these words is sweeter than music to those who have the spirit of Christ.

Not only does private prayer become more efficacious when it acquires this character, but participation in the greatest prayer of all, the Mass, becomes more fruitful. For then is carried out what St. Gregory the Great expresses with such pith and power when he says: "We who celebrate the mysteries of our Lord's Passion ought to imitate what we celebrate."

5

His Cross And Human Pride

It is obvious that anyone who would seek to commune with God through prayer, while having a heart filled with pride, would be rebuffed. Christ told the parable of the Pharisee and the publican in the temple to emphasize this truth. Because God withstands the proud, the first step in approaching him is acknowledgment of one's inferiority and unworthiness.

Christ's doctrine probably would be much more acceptable to certain types of people if it did not place such emphasis on the need for humility. Those who take themselves and their abilities too seriously are often willing to accept what they call the Christian ethic, but they seem to wish that the last chapters of the four Gospels had never been written. They refuse to accept "the scandal of the cross."

Some of those who reject the Savior probably would accept him if he had given his life for mankind surrounded with a little glamour. They might have a different attitude toward him if, for example, he had allowed himself to be killed leading his followers in battle. Christ knew that the cross would be a scandal to the proud, as he knew that the cross would be a scandal to his Apostles when he warned them Holy Thursday night that they would all be scandalized in him once he had allowed himself to be taken captive by his enemies.

Christianity cannot be fragmentized, and those who reject the cross as a scandal reject Christ, and to reject Christ is to reject God. The complete Christian, far from being ashamed of the cross, says with St. Paul: "We ought to glory in the cross of our Lord Jesus Christ, in which is our salvation, resurrection, and life" (cf. Gal. 6:14).

God will be accepted only on his own terms. And he has shown his terms by placing the cross at the very center of the universe. The cross stands for "the humility of God." Man's acceptance of the humility of God entails man's humbling of himself. "Have this mind among yourselves," wrote St. Paul, "which was in Christ Jesus, who, though he was in the form of God, did not count equality with God a thing to be grasped, but emptied himself, taking the form of a servant. . . . And being found in human form he humbled himself and became obedient unto death, even death on a cross" (Phil. 2:5–8).

In saying that Christ humbles himself *even* to death on a cross, St. Paul is implying that this is the extreme of humiliation. When the wicked are portrayed in the Book of Wisdom as plotting the persecution of the just man "because he is contrary to our doings," their final decision is: "Let us condemn him to a most shameful death." The proud Romans considered death on the cross so shameful that they forbade the crucifixion of any citizen of the empire, even the most criminal.

The evil plotters described in the Book of Wisdom thus found their counterparts in the last priests of the Old Law who on Calvary could not conceal their satisfaction in having had their long-awaited and now-unrecognized Messiah condemned to the most shameful of deaths. It is not unlikely that they were thinking of the words of their own Scriptures: "God's curse rests on him who hangs on a tree," and they probably planned to quote this text to discredit Christ's claim to be the Son of God.

Not only was the Crucifixion unimaginably humiliating in itself, but circumstance was piled on circumstance to add to the ignominy of it. The cross was placed between the crosses of two common criminals. It was raised on a small hill near two of the busiest gates to the city of Jerusalem. At midday a multitude of travelers would have been passing along the busy road that was so near Calvary, and the Gospels indicate that many of the passersby stopped to join the chorus of mockery and blasphemy directed at the crucified King of kings.

What a spectacle for the angelic hosts to gaze upon! The spittle from the soldiers' filthy mouths is in the beard of him whose countenance in heaven had blinded them with its glory. The mock crown of thorns is on the head of their eternal King. The nails hold fast the hands of him whom they had watched sending stars and planets whirling through space. Jeers and taunts are spewed at him before whom they had bowed in adoration and cried: "Holy, Holy, Holy!"

Isaiah had prophesied that the Messiah would appear as "despised and rejected by men . . . one from whom men hide their faces . . . stricken, smitten by God, and afflicted" (Is. 53:3–4). And David had Christ say to His eternal Father: "In thee our fathers trusted; they trusted, and thou didst deliver them. . . . But I am a worm, and no man; scorned by men, and despised by the people. All who see me mock at me, they make mouths at me, they wag their heads; 'He committed his cause to the Lord; let him deliver him, let him rescue him, for he delights in him!' " (Ps. 22:4, 6–8). Those who had originally heard these prophecies concerning the humiliation of Christ could hardly have had any idea of what the reality would be.

The Gothic Missal of Spain contains a preface with the words: "Such indeed is the importance of humility to man that the very majesty of God taught it by his own example." And there is a prayer in one of the votive Masses and the prayer of the Mass of Palm Sunday which begins: "Almighty and eternal God, who, to give the human race an example of humility, didst have our Savior assume our flesh and undergo the cross. . . ."

St. Bernard wondered how anybody could fail to humble himself after considering the humility of Christ: "Shame on you, proud ashes! God abases himself and do you exalt yourself? God subjects himself to me, and do you, eager to lord it over them, set yourself above your Creator? For as often as I desire preeminence over men, so often do I strive to excel God. . . . If you disdain, O man, to follow the example of man, at least you can follow your Creator without dishonor."

But those who are overly impressed with their own very finite minds will not accept a God who humbled himself and asks them to do likewise. They will not see that "the stone which the builders

rejected has become the cornerstone." The proud begin by refus-
ing to see and they end by being unable to see. Pride creates a
vicious circle. Its refusal to see prevents those who are guilty of it
from kneeling before God to ask for the grace to see.

To those who totally accept Christ, the cross is not "foolishness,"
as St. Paul said it was to the Gentiles, nor is it to them "a stumbling
block," as he said it was to the Jews. The danger for those who
believe is that, while accepting the humility of the crucified Christ
with their minds, they will fail to mirror his humility in their lives.
St. Augustine reminds the followers of Christ that our Savior did
not say that they were to learn of him how to create a world or to
work miracles, but to learn of him to be meek and humble of
heart.

One of the most difficult aspects of Christianity for Paul to
accept when be stopped being Saul, the proud Pharisee, must have
been Christ's doctrine of humility. But he was to embrace it so
wholeheartedly that he could write: "I am satisfied, for Christ's
sake . . . with insults . . . with persecutions, with distresses." He
absorbed the wisdom of the cross so completely that he found joy
in being humbled after the example of his Master. "Gladly," he
wrote, "will I glory in my infirmities, that the strength of Christ
may dwell in me."

Another striking example of finding joy in being humbled is
that of St. Francis of Assisi, whose humility kept him from accepting ordination to the priesthood. One bitterly cold winter day, St.
Francis and his faithful companion, Bro. Leo, were on a journey to
a friary of the order. St. Francis called to Bro. Leo, who was walk-
ing ahead, and said to him: "Bro. Leo, if it were to please God that
the Friars Minor should give, in all lands, a great example of holiness and edification, write down and note carefully, that this would
not be perfect joy." A little farther on, St. Francis called on Bro. Leo
again and said that if the Friars were to make the lame to walk,
give sight to the blind, hearing to the deaf, and to perform all sorts
of other miracles, Leo should write down that this would not be
perfect joy.

This went on until Francis had enumerated all the greatest tal-
ents, gifts, and graces, adding each time that Bro. Leo should write

down that possessing them would not be perfect joy. Bro. Leo, eager to know what Francis was leading up to, asked him to come to the point and say wherein was perfect joy. Francis replied that if, when they arrived at the friary, all drenched with rain and shivering from the cold, covered with mud and exhausted with hunger, the porter, taking them for impostors, were to refuse to let them in, this would be perfect joy. And if, having found the cold and hunger unbearable, they should knock again, and the porter were to rush out and throw them to the ground in the snow and beat them with a knotted stick, this would be perfect joy.

Just as there are religious orders founded to emphasize by their title and particular work some aspect of Catholicism, so God raises up saints to spotlight some particular virtue. Another man who specialized in humility and humiliation was St. Benedict Joseph Labre, the layman who became a wanderer through Europe, not because he liked wandering but because such a life afforded so many opportunities for humiliation. He used to visit one of his favorite churches near the Trajan Forum in Rome, although he knew that urchins would be waiting there to pelt him with stones and throw him in the mud that covered the forum. No doubt, many think that a man of this sort is not only odd but fit for an asylum. But his was the perfect logic of the cross.

St. Bernard went to the heart of the need for humility when he said: "Our heart is a vessel destined to receive grace; in order that it may contain grace in abundance it must be empty of self-love and vainglory. When humility has there prepared a vast capacity to be filled, grace flows in, for there is a close affinity between grace and humility."

Christ came that we might have life, that life which is called grace. There is no room for this life in a soul that is filled with pride. Room can be made only by the process of digging out self-complacency. This process is so important to man that the God-Man endured the incredible humiliation of the cross to teach it to him.

6

His Cross And Material Goods

Detachment from inordinate feelings of self-esteem is the first step in what may be called the emptying process which marks the beginning of spiritual living. But when a person has detached himself from self-complacency, there may remain attachment to worldly things. Any earthly attachment that interferes with our attachment to God must be ruthlessly sacrificed.

Sometimes pagans or unbelievers give a striking example of natural virtue. A thought-provoking and charming story is told about the famous Greek philosopher, Socrates, as he passed through the marketplace at Athens one day. On display was a seemingly endless supply of merchandise. In stalls were mounds of fruits and vegetables from outlying farms. Bolts of rich fabrics were piled high, or spread out for inspection. Above the chatter of buyers and sellers could be heard the sounds of livestock. Looking around at the vast display, Socrates exclaimed: "What a lot of things I don't need!"

Today the hucksters come into the living room through television and radio, and they use the weirdest means to persuade people to use, or increase their use of, products without which their grandparents were able to be happy. They will try to convince their captive audience by adapting a classical Strauss waltz to some jingle about dog food. Or some cavernous outer-space voice will come booming forth solemnly to announce the fabulous qualities of a breakfast food. Or they will fracture grammar in contending that nobody, *but* nobody, sells as cheaply as Bimble's or that Old Bronze tastes *like* a cigarette should. They want all within earshot to increase their use of earthly goods so that they may give the hucksters the means of increasing *their* use of earthly goods.

At this late stage in the era of the sky-is-the-limit standard of living, it is more or less generally conceded that an increase of earthly goods does not mean an increase in happiness. No people ever had more material abundance, but along with this worldly prosperity goes a profound moral and spiritual emptiness.

Every man has to decide what his general attitude toward material things will be. As the God-Man, Christ teaches mankind from the cross the proper attitude toward worldly possessions.

Through the Word, the Second Person of the Trinity who was made flesh, according to St. John, "all things were made . . . and without him was not anything made that was made" (John 1:3). Through him, therefore, the world, with all its riches, was created. When he came into his world, he could have brought all its wealth to his feet. But, by coming in the unheard-of poverty of a stable, he gave a hint of the use he would make of the material riches he had brought into being.

He willed to live in poverty during the thirty-three years between the cave and the cross. But here we are considering the incredible poverty of the cross. The man on the cross is the Son of God, and he has been stripped! Men see so many representations of the Crucifixion that they take it and the circumstances surrounding it for granted. They have become so accustomed to the fact that God-made-man died naked on the cross that they do not give it a second thought.

It is significant that crucifixion appears to be the only form of execution in which the one executed is stripped. A man is not stripped if he is shot, hanged, or beheaded. The completeness of the stripping of our Savior is indicated by the description of the disposal of his garments. St. John writes: "When the soldiers had crucified Jesus they took his garments and made four parts, one for each soldier; also his tunic. But the tunic was without seam, woven from top to bottom; so they said to one another, 'Let us not tear it, but cast lots for it to see whose it shall be' " (John 19:23–24).

David, in prophecy, had foretold that the Redeemer would thus be stripped, and the Gospels recall this by stating that the Scripture was being fulfilled: "They divide my garments among them, and for my raiment they cast lots" (Ps. 22:18). It was no accident that the God who had created all things allowed himself to be divested of everything earthly, even the garments with which he had clothed his sacred humanity.

His garments were not even turned over to his Mother, a gesture that the most common decency demanded. A more complete divesting of earthly goods is inconceivable. There is in this stripping a total rejection of the things of this world by him who created the world. The question that must be answered is what Christ is teaching mankind in this facet of the mystery of the cross.

This was obviously the divine Master's way of teaching the blessedness of the spirit of poverty. From the pulpit of the cross, he was underscoring what he had preached from the Mount of the Beatitudes: "Do not lay up for yourselves treasures on earth, where moth and rust consume, and where thieves break through and steal; but lay up for yourselves treasures in heaven, where neither rust nor moth consumes, and where thieves do not break in and steal."

The first man and woman abused the gifts of creation. The fall of man demanded that mankind have a different attitude toward created goods than that which would have prevailed had not things gone awry in the Garden of Eden. Through the fall, there arose in man, along with other unhealthy and ungodly desires, the lust of the eyes, that is, greed for earthly possessions. This greed gives rise to a passionate search for worldly goods. In some it becomes so great that it leads them to lie and cheat and steal and kill, as is evident from the reports of the journalistic exploiters of the world's daily burden of sin. The same greed often causes the wealthy to forget that they are the stewards of God's bounty, and thus harden their hearts toward their needy fellowman.

It was to show how mistaken is such an attitude toward the goods of this world that he who came as Redeemer and Teacher of mankind willed to divest himself, on the cross, of every last earthly thing.

God who looked on his creation in the beginning, according to Genesis, and found it good, did not find it bad when he came to redeem the world. Man had merely misused the good things that

God had placed on earth for his use during his journey to eternity, and God would put worldly goods in their proper perspective through the wisdom of the cross.

It is heretical to hold that there is anything bad in the material goods with which God has stocked the earth. The badness comes only when these good things are abused. Man can use what God has placed in the world as much as be wishes, but the cross tells him to do it in such a way that the use of these things will not harm but help him and others in time and eternity.

It is, of course, not surprising that the stripping of himself by the Lord of creation should have led millions of men and women throughout the ages to strip themselves of worldly possessions by the vow of poverty. One of the hundreds of thousands who would follow the Savior in rejecting even legitimate earthly possessions was Francis of Assisi, whose love of poverty was to become a great religious romance. His complete oneness with the crucified was indicated by his receiving in his body the wounds of Christ. The first public step in this union was also a dramatic stripping.

Francis had been hailed to the court of the bishop of Assisi where his father accused him of giving away money and food to the poor, and of using certain of his possessions to obtain money for stones with which he was rebuilding a church that had fallen into disrepair. Francis did not deny any of this. He merely stripped himself of the clothes which he had received from his father, placed them at his feet, and announced that henceforth he would have no father but his Father in heaven.

Nothing could make it clearer that this stripping of earthly goods involves no contempt for the bounty of a benign Creator. Francis is known outside the Church, unfortunately, more for his love of God's creation than for his greater love of the cross. It is true that few have been as eloquent as he in praising the Lord for Mother Earth, Brother Sun, Sister Water. But it is also true that it would be difficult to find, even among saints, one more closely identified with the crucified Christ. Like all others who have stripped themselves in this way, he was only showing his determination to keep worldly goods in their proper perspective.

The whole meaning of the stripping of Christ is summed up

concisely in the beautiful words of St. Paul: "For you know the graciousness of our Lord Jesus Christ—how, being rich, he became poor for your sake, that by his poverty you might become rich." He stripped himself of earthly riches that men might be clothed in spiritual and eternal riches.

It is really all a question of detachment and attachment. One of the most common terms in spiritual literature is *detachment*. It would be a good idea if we always talked about attachment when talking about detachment. Man cannot be totally detached, just as he cannot be suspended in space. He must be attached to something. If a man lives according to the wisdom of the cross, he will not be attached to material things in such a way that he becomes absorbed by them, and thus loses sight of those of eternity. Guided by this wisdom, he will practice at least that detachment from worldly possessions which leaves him free to be attached mainly to God and to the divine riches which he bestows so lavishly.

7

His Cross And A Sense Of Sin

Even when one has made some progress in humility and detachment from earthly goods, temptations of the flesh will persist. The youthful St. Gabriel suffered such temptations on his deathbed. The heroic Curé of Ars experienced violent temptations against purity, even after he had made giant strides in the love of God. One of the best ways of conquering such temptations is the cultivation of a sense of sin.

There can be no doubt at all that the weakening of a sense of sin has kept pace with the playing down of the cross by many who still call themselves Christians. This playing down of the cross is sometimes done even by those who claim to have received a call to preach the Gospel. A minister in New York, for example, ironically used Good Friday as an occasion for protesting against vivid descriptions of the Crucifixion of our Lord. His argument was that the Evangelists had discreetly passed over the brutal details of the Passion. He ignored the fact that Christian preaching is nothing else than a commentary on the Gospel and an interpretation of it. The Evangelists omitted many details which we try to fill in.

Wisdom dictates that all possible means be used to overcome the temptations which are part of man's earthly trial. And there is no stronger argument against succumbing to temptation than the thought of what man's consenting to temptation did to the Son of God on the cross. St. Paul states that those who give way to temptation crucify again to themselves the Savior of the world.

He tells his readers what a deterrent from sin the thought of the cross should be when he says that "if we sin willfully after receiving the truth, there remains no longer sacrifice for sins, but a certain dreadful expectation of judgment. . . . A man making void the

Law of Moses dies without any mercy on the word of two or three witnesses: How much worse punishments do you think he deserves who has trodden underfoot the Son of God, and has regarded as unclean the blood of the covenant through which he was sanctified?"

A number of years ago, a surgeon made a reverent study of the incredible agonies of crucifixion. Dr. Pierre Barbet calls attention to the torture of cramp, which is probably just one of the torments that has escaped attention in meditating on the cross. Dr. Barbet says: "It is like a wounded man suffering from tetanus, a prey to those horrible spasms which once seen can never be forgotten. It is what we describe as *tetanization*, when the cramps become generalized. . . . His breathing has become shorter and lighter. . . . The air enters with a whistling sound, but scarcely comes out any longer. He is breathing in the upper regions only. He breathes in a little but cannot breathe out. He thirsts for air. (It is like someone in the throes of asthma.)

"A flush has gradually spread over his pale face; it has turned a violent purple and then blue. He is *asphyxiating*. His lungs which are filled with air can no longer empty themselves. His forehead is covered with sweat. His eyes are prominent and rolling. What an appalling pain must be hammering in his head!

"Slowly, with a superhuman effort, he is using the nail through his feet as a fulcrum—that is to say, he is pressing on his wounds... the breathing becomes more ample and moves down to a lower level. . . . Why is he making all this effort? It is in order to speak to us! 'Father, forgive them.' Yes, may he forgive us, who are his executioners. But a moment later his body begins to sink down once more . . . and the tetanization will come on again.

"And each time that he speaks and each time he wishes to breathe, it will be necessary for him to strengthen himself, to get his breath back, holding himself upright on the nail through his feet. And each movement has its echo, in his hands, in inexpressible pain. It is a question of periodical asphyxiation of the poor unfortunate who is being strangled and then allowed to come back to life, to be choked once more."

Added to such unspeakable physical torture is the mental desolation reflected in the cry of the dying Savior, "My God, my God,
why hast thou forsaken me?" St. Paul had such a picture in mind
when he wrote to the Galatians: "O foolish Galatians! Who has
bewitched you before whom Jesus Christ has been depicted crucified?"

The impact that the thought of the Crucifixion can have on a
Catholic conscience is brought out in a powerful passage in
Brideshead Revisited by Evelyn Waugh. Brideshead, the eldest brother in the English Catholic family about which the novel revolves,
forces his sister to face the gravity of the situation in which she has
placed herself by marrying one divorced man and consorting with
another. The bombshell is a seemingly casual remark which
Brideshead makes to his sister in the presence of the latter of the
two men about "living in sin." Her companion in sin tries to persuade her not to pay any attention to her brother's remark, but she
admits that her brother is right. She tells him what sin means to a
conscientious Catholic: "Christ dying with it, nailed hand and
foot; hanging over the bed in the night nursery; hanging year after
year in the dark little study at Farm Street with the shining oil-
cloth; hanging in the dark church where only the old charwoman
raises the dust and one candle burns; hanging at noon among the
crowds and the soldiers; no comfort but a sponge of vinegar and
the kind words of a thief; hanging forever; never the cool sepul-
chre and the grave's clothes spread on the stone slab, never the oil
and spices in the dark cave; always the midday sun and the dice
clicking for the seamless coat."

No state is worse than that of those who, through habitual sinning, have lost a sense of sin. The safest way to avoid such a state is
to cultivate a consciousness of sin such as the saints developed.
Nobody can fail to see that the saints, who are the only complete
Christians, derived their overwhelming sense of sin mainly from
the contemplation of the crucified. Their realization of the
heinousness of sin grew with their understanding of the meaning
of the cross. *Were You There When They Crucified My Lord?* We were
not there physically, but there is a timelessness about the

Crucifixion, and one can be there constantly in spirit. Going there frequently in spirit is the best possible way to prepare for those inevitable temptations which can be occasions of either loss or gain both for time and for eternity.

8

His Cross And Combat

Having a sense of sin does not mean that one will have no struggle in overcoming temptation. A person could have a monumental hatred of the evil of sin, and still have to fight its seductiveness. In the cross, Christ not only shows man the black malice of sin, but gives him an example of the fortitude and even heroism which are required in the battle with evil.

It is unfortunate that the world's greatest hero is so often portrayed as a dainty, posturing figure, whose face, except for the beard, could be that of Mary Magdalen. Such portrayals represent the grossest distortion. These caricatures are passed out as representations of him who persuaded the gnarled, rock-ribbed Peter and the Sons of Thunder to leave all and follow him on ten seconds' notice. It has been observed that, if the Savior had looked like these vapid travesties, he could never have endured the savage tortures of his Passion.

An unbeliever could hardly be blamed for failing to see behind such parodies the greatest hero who ever lived, a hero whose exploits make those of other heroes, real or fictional, look rather puny. Within the Church, one of the effects of such false portrayals of the world's Redeemer is that those who are raised on such fare will find it difficult to visualize Christ as their heroic leader in the combat which forms such a large part of earthly life.

In the Old Testament, Job stated that *"the life of man on earth is a warfare."* And that warrior, St. Paul, never allowed the first members of the Church to forget that they were part of the fighting Church, the *Church Militant.* Writing to one of the leaders in the Church's battle, Timothy, he urged him to *"fight the good fight of faith."* He recalled to the recipients of his letters the great battlers

49

for God who had preceded them, and the example of their heroic captain, whose main battle was fought and won on Calvary's height.

"Therefore, let us also," he wrote to the Hebrews, "having such a cloud of witnesses over us, put away every encumbrance and the sin entangling us, and *run with patience to the fight* set before us, looking toward the author and finisher of faith, Jesus, who . . . endured a cross." He reminds them that, unlike their Master, they "have not yet resisted unto blood in the struggle with sin."

There used to be a television program called *Greatest Fights of the Century*, the heroes of which were boxers, remembered and revered by a scattering of men of the older generations. In a few decades, hardly anybody will remember them. But *the Fight of the Centuries*, fought on a small hill outside Jerusalem nineteen hundred years ago, is kept in daily remembrance, without the help of television, by hundreds of millions of men and women. And the hero of that fight is loved and adored, in the literal sense of these words, by people everywhere, and will be so held in affection and reverence, not only until the end of the world, but through the endless ages of eternity.

This fight was prepared for on the Mount of Olives, where our heroic captain made a last-minute study of the plans for the most decisive battle in human history. There he saw that victory could be achieved only when he had fallen mortally wounded. Having completed his plans and preparation, he plunged into the fray by saying to his Apostles: "Rise, let us go. Behold, he who betrays me is at hand."

We show little discernment if we suppose that it was easier for Christ to endure the cross than it would be for us to go through such a harrowing ordeal. Let us not suppose that his being God blunted the edges of the pain that pressed in on him from every side. His divinity and the perfection of the human nature which he had united in his Godhead only sharpened the atrocious torture of his Crucifixion. It can be said that, because he was God, he suffered the agony of Crucifixion twice. On the Mount of Olives, where he envisioned every brutal detail of what awaited him so vividly that he sweat blood, he was crucified in mind and soul. On

Mount Calvary, the savage torments from which he had recoiled in Gethsemane became a bloody reality.

That Christ endured the cross while innocent makes his heroism all the greater. People generally accept with stoicism suffering which they have brought on themselves. An illustration of this attitude is found in the remarkably frank statement of the Good Thief to his companion on the other cross: "We receive what our deeds deserve." St. Peter refers to this acceptance of suffering on the part of the guilty when he says: "For what is the glory if, when you sin and are buffeted, you endure it?" He then goes on to emphasize that Christ left us an example of suffering while innocent, recalling the prophecy of Isaiah concerning the Redeemer, "Who did no sin, neither was deceit found in his mouth."

Another factor that throws the heroism of our Lord into greater relief is that he not only offered his life for others, but sacrificed it for those who were unworthy. St. Paul makes note of this when he writes: "Scarcely in behalf of a just man does one die; yet perhaps one might bring himself to die for a good man. But . . . when as yet we were sinners, Christ died for us."

It is hardly surprising that the Church which sprang from the bleeding side of her heroic Savior should have sent marching down the ages an unending procession of heroic men, women, and children. Imitators of the fortitude of Christ have come from every class. His Church has given the world heroic apostles and martyrs, heroic popes, bishops, and priests, heroic founders of religious orders, heroic monks and nuns, heroic kings and peasants, heroic statesmen, physicians, writers, and artisans, heroic husbands, wives, and children.

Relatively few are called on to display courage on a grand scale, as have thousands of heroic members of the Church in Europe and Asia who have come face to face with the diabolical evil of Communism. But no follower of Christ should either expect or desire to escape occasions when courage, and even heroism, will be called for.

Temptations and trials are always lurking around the corner, even for those who lead the most humdrum lives. These tests are met best by those who keep their eyes on their heroic leader on the cross. The thought of the fortitude which he showed helps those who bear it in mind to avoid the shame of acting cowardly in the battle in which we are all engaged in his name.

9

His Cross And Human Hope

A person who has had the misfortune to fall into sin can make two serious mistakes. The first is to lose hope of being forgiven. This is the sin of despair. The second is to go on sinning, presuming that God is too merciful to let him die in his sin. This is the sin of presumption. Hope lies between these two extremes.

One of the most striking facts about Calvary is that no word of rebuke fell from the lips of the crucified Christ. He had often rebuked men for their irreligion, injustice, and hypocrisy during his public ministry. But there was not even a hint of condemnation now that he hung from the cross. We see on Calvary none of that divine anger which caused him to drive the moneychangers from the Temple. We hear none of those dreaded judgments in which he told men to their faces that they were full of robbery and wickedness. We hear from the cross no reference to whited sepulchers and broods of vipers.

This absence of denunciation on Calvary is all the more striking because there were so many manifestations of wickedness that appeared to deserve immediate retribution. There was the greed of the soldiers who were throwing dice for his garments. There was the blasphemy of one of the thieves crucified with him. There was the relentless hatred of the chief priests. There was the stark injustice of his Crucifixion. There was the enormous crime of deicide.

If those standing about the cross were waiting for thunderous words of rebuke for the awful vices that manifested themselves, they were waiting in vain. This day was to become known forever as *Good* Friday because God's goodness and mercy stand out in the sharpest relief from the cross of the divine Redeemer. Judgment will surely come later, but God wills that his mercy, rather than his justice, shine from Calvary's height.

St. John was to write in his Gospel that "God did not send his Son into the world in order to judge the world, but that the world might be saved through him." He wrote this in commenting on Christ's words to Nicodemus: "And as Moses lifted up the serpent in the desert, even so must the Son of Man be lifted up, that those who believe in him may not perish, but may have life everlasting."

The Son of Man is now lifted up, and he is making it clear that he is using the cross not as a judgment-seat, but as a mercy-seat. Instead of thunderbolts of divine wrath, there are the most moving offers of divine forgiveness. And so, the very first word that the Savior utters from the cross is not one of condemnation or reproach, but that prayer of forgiveness which never fails to stir us after ten thousand hearings. Out over the harsh jeering and blaspheming of his enemies floats like a strain of masterful music the most touching utterance the world has ever heard: "Father, forgive them, for they know not what they do."

Calvary signifies the dawn of hope for an otherwise doomed race. This is why our Redeemer will utter no word of reproach from the cross. He wills that an atmosphere of hope pervade Calvary. He wants to make it clear that the cross is the fulfillment of the words of the prophet Jeremiah: "This is the covenant that I will make with the House of Israel after those days, says the Lord: I will put my law within them and I will write it in their hearts, and I will be their God and they will be my people, for I will forgive their iniquity and I will remember their sins no more."

Because of the cross, Christianity is a religion of hope. There would be no hope for mankind if it were not for the cross. The cross is *spes unica*, the only hope of a fallen race. The destiny of mankind is eternal life with God, but there would be no hope of achieving that destiny if the human race had not been redeemed from its burdens of sin through the cross.

It is clear that the divine Redeemer is telling the world that his offering of himself on the cross is mankind's greatest opportunity to obtain forgiveness for its many and great crimes. This is the amnesty of the human race. On Calvary, the saving rain of God's forgiveness falls into the receptive hearts of the Good Thief and the centurion, who receive it as the parched earth receives the blessed rain from the skies. It falls into the hearts of those who will shortly leave Calvary striking their breasts in repentance.

In the days ahead, the saving rain of God's mercy will fall into the hearts of thousands of Jews who will hear from the Apostles the good news of their redemption through Christ's saving cross. Throughout the centuries, the rain of forgiveness will fall into the heart of every man who will open his heart to receive it.

The hope of mankind was dashed by the sin of Adam, but was raised immediately by the promise of a Redeemer. Now on Calvary the promise becomes a reality. The cross is the answer to those who are quoted by Isaiah as saying: "The Lord has forsaken me, and the Lord has forgotten me." Christ replies through his cross: "Can a woman forget her infant, so as not to have pity on the son of her womb? And if she should forget, yet I will not forget thee."

Christ bears the hopes of humanity in his outstretched arms on the cross. With that gesture of embrace he encourages every creature of his hands to hope. Moses in a canticle speaks as though he were standing before the cross when he says: "As the eagle incites its young to fly by hovering over its brood, so he spread his wings to receive them and carried them on his shoulders" (cf. Deut. 32:11). The divine eagle of Calvary is powerful enough to receive and carry on his world-covering wings the hopes of the whole human race.

This is the outpouring of hope concerning which St. Paul wrote to Titus: "But when the goodness and loving kindness of God our Savior appeared, he saved us, not because of deeds done by us in righteousness, but in virtue of his own mercy, by the washing of regeneration and renewal in the Holy Spirit, which he poured out upon us richly through Jesus Christ our Savior, so that we might be justified by his grace and become heirs in hope of eternal life" (Titus 3:4–7).

On the cross, all the Savior's great parables of mercy are underscored. From the cross, the Good Shepherd sweeps with his gaze the wide world, counting his sheep and praying that they will see and heed the beacon of hope that has been erected here at the center of the earth. Like a most forgiving father, the Redeemer looks to the farthest horizon, praying that his prodigal sons will see his arms outstretched to welcome them.

Only two things can directly destroy hope. One is the sin of despair, which is committed by those who give up hope of having their sins forgiven and reaching eternal life. The other is the sin of presumption, which is committed by those who indulge in false hope and foolishly suppose that no matter what they do, everything will turn out all right in the end.

Those who despair question one of God's attributes—his mercy. They dare to set a limit to God's forgiveness when he himself has placed no limit to it. To commit the sin of despair, a person has to lie to himself about God's willingness to forgive. He has to deceive himself in the face of the mountain of evidence which the world's Redeemer built up on Calvary.

What Dante saw inscribed over the entrance to hell—"All hope abandon, ye who enter here"—may be inscribed over the dark caverns entered by those who give themselves over to the sin that caused Judas to climax his other crimes with suicide. This sin appears to be closely linked with pride. Those who commit it appear to be boasting that in the field of sin at least they are outstanding—so outstanding that even God cannot forgive them.

Presumption is the sin committed by those whose hope is baseless because they are living in such a way as to make themselves unworthy of the eternal life for which they claim to hope. The presumptuous attempt to take a mean advantage of God's goodness and mercy. They go on in their life of sin, telling themselves that God is too good to let them die in sin.

Those who are guilty of presumption make a mockery of God's law. If they were right in supposing that God would not allow anyone to die in sin, it would not make any difference whether one kept God's law or broke it. A person could commit every kind of crime and feel that in the end it would not matter because he would be snatched from the brink of hell regardless of what he had done. It is evident that self-deception is a factor in the sin of presumption, just as it is in the sin of despair.

Those who, avoiding the extremes of presumption and despair, practice true hope, will see in the cross the instrument and symbol of this virtue.

10

His Cross And Penance

Hope is such a precious possession to sinful mankind that it is particularly reprehensible to abuse this virtue. It is abused when one expects to be pardoned for one's sins without sincerely repenting of them. The sincerity of a man's repentance can be gauged by his willingness to do penance. Just as the word *penance* comes from the word *repentance*, so the performance of penance is an effect of repentance.

The Church insists, in the face of a self-indulgent human nature, not only that man repent of his sins, but that he do penance for them. This insistence of the Church on the necessity for penance is another confirmation of the truth of her claim to be the one Church established by him who said: "Unless you do penance, you shall all likewise perish."

The Catholic Church has a great corps of men and women who are specialists in penance. She has dotted the earth with monasteries and convents where members of penitential orders engage in fasts, vigils, and expiatory prayer. She encourages her professed penitents to offer their lives as a living oblation in union with the supreme oblation of the cross. But she expects all her members to share in the expiation which she offers in union with her divine head for the sins of mankind.

All mankind is involved in the Passion, even though many men reject this idea. The majority of men are like a group of singers who one time participated in a rendition in English of Bach's *Passion According to St. John*. The day after the recital, the music critic of a daily paper praised the tenor who had sung the part of the Evangelist for conveying a sense of the drama of the Passion. Of the performance as a whole, however, the critic said that, while it often gave musical pleasure, "it did not inspire what Bach intended, a sense of reverence." The performers would have stared in wonderment if they had been urged by the conductor to feel a personal relationship toward the events described by St. John. The momentous truth that every man is involved in the Passion would have been foreign to their thinking.

Sometimes people will stand before a crucifix of fine craftsmanship and exclaim on its beauty. They do this in a detached way, as though they were viewing some work of art toward which they felt no individual relationship. They are like those who passed along the road that ran near Calvary on that first Good Friday afternoon. One can see these wayfarers glancing casually toward the three crosses, remarking that three more wretched human beings were dying as criminals. Their eyes probably lingered for a moment on the figure of the famous preacher and wonder-worker from Nazareth. But this figure meant little or nothing to them personally. As they continued along the road, one to his noontime meal, another to his afternoon business, still another to his siesta, they acted as though they were not involved at all in the Crucifixion of the Son of God.

It is impossible to understand the Church's policy of penance unless one realizes one's personal involvement in the Passion of Christ. The Church reminds her members of their share in the Passion in the *Reproaches* which she puts on the lips of Christ during the adoration of the cross on Good Friday:

> My people, what have I done to thee?
> Or in what have I grieved thee?
> Answer me.
> Because I fed thee with manna, and brought
>   thee into a land exceedingly good, thou
>   hast prepared a cross for thy Savior.
> I gave thee a royal scepter, and thou
>   hast given me a crown of thorns.

I opened the sea before thee: and thou
    with a spear hast opened my side.
I have exalted thee with great power, and thou
    hast hanged me on the gibbet of the cross.

His flesh was lacerated. It was pierced with thorns and dug with nails. There was a harrowing of that perfect body which appears to be beyond all endurance. As for indulgence of appetites, the impression is given that no food passed the lips of Christ once his Passion began. Scripture says that he refused the wine which was offered to him on a sponge at the height of his agony. The thirst which was the result of the Crucifixion parched his lips and mouth and whole body so dreadfully that it was the only physical torment which caused him to utter anything approaching complaint.

There was no plea for a loosening of the nails, which caused such paroxysms of agony, and which held him in that brutally cramped position for three hours. There was no cry for the removal of the thorns which continued to burn into his sacred head. There was no call for a sponge over his flesh to wipe away the drying blood and sweat. There was just that brief, heartrending cry: "I thirst!" (John 19:28). And even this was not so much a plea for relief as a statement of fact wrung from his human nature.

St. Bernard says it is a shameful thing to be a delicate member under a thorn-crowned head. Christ himself warned that it is not only shameful to shun penance, but dangerous to one's eternal salvation. "The men of Nineveh," he said, "will rise in the judgment with this generation, and will condemn it; for they repented at the preaching of Jonah, and behold a greater than Jonah is here." Christ is referring to the dramatic way in which the inhabitants of the great city of Nineveh averted through penance the dire punishments with which they had been threatened by Jonah because of their wickedness. The prophet had warned that, unless they repented, their city would be destroyed in forty days. Scripture records that "the men of Nineveh believed in God and they proclaimed a great fast."

The king of Nineveh issued a proclamation: "Let neither men nor beasts taste anything. And let men cry to the Lord with all their strength, and let them turn everyone from his evil way. Who can tell if God will turn and forgive. . . . And God saw their works, that they were turned from their evil way: and God had mercy with regard to the evil which he said he would do to them, and he did it not."

Another outstanding pre-Christian example that confounds the follower of Christ who shirks penance is found in the Book of Judith. Holy Scripture says that the Assyrian armies of the time "covered the face of the earth like locusts," threatening the Israelites with complete destruction. "The whole nation made appeal to the Lord, doing penance . . . with fast and prayer."

The people of Israel were saved when Judith went into the camp of Holofernes, the commander of the Assyrian forces, and cut off his head while he was in a drunken stupor. Scripture indicates the source of her strength when it says that "she wore sackcloth . . . and fasted all the days of her life, except the Sabbaths . . . and the feasts of the House of Israel." St. Ambrose marveled that "the fast of one woman overthrew the countless armies of the Assyrians." Judith will also rise in the Judgment to condemn any Christians who shunned penance because before their eyes "Jesus Christ has been depicted crucified." St. Ambrose says that penance is not only a sacrifice of reconciliation, but also a means for gaining strength to overcome temptation. St. Bede says that the most grievous trials, whether from unclean spirits or from men, are overcome by fasting and prayer.

That there are evils which cannot be overcome without prayer and fasting is indicated by an incident in the Gospels. Christ had given his Apostles power to cast out devils, but on one occasion they found themselves powerless to deliver a boy who was possessed. Appeal had to be made to the Master. After he had freed the boy from the evil spirit, the Apostles asked him why they had not been able to do so. Christ told them that "there is no way of casting out such spirits as this except by prayer and fasting."

In the great apparitions of the Mother of God in modern times, she has made it clear that the punishments deserved by a guilty world can be warded off only through prayer and penance. In a moving exchange between the Mother of Christ and the children to whom she appeared at Fátima, she showed vividly the way in which mankind's penances are accepted by the Almighty.

The children had found a rope which because of its rough texture was irritating to the skin. They divided it among them and wore pieces next to their young flesh. The Queen of Heaven did not consider such an act of penance beneath her notice. She told the children that God was pleased with this act of reparation, but that he did not want them to wear the rope to bed. Here is the Most High at one time answering those who think that he cannot be bothered noticing the small details of human lives, and telling man that many such acts of penance build up a dam which serves to hold back the torrent of punishment overhanging the human race.

The Archangel Raphael explained to Tobit the wonderful effects of fasting when it is united with good works and prayer. "Prayer is good when accompanied by fasting, almsgiving, and righteousness," he said. "It is better to give alms than to treasure up gold" (Tob. 12:8). This is a reminder that penance which is not accompanied by the practice of the other virtues is unacceptable.

Penance which is not joined with an effort to keep God's law is a contradiction of the spirit from which true penance proceeds. St. Bede says that "to fast, in a general sense, is not only to abstain from meat, but to restrain oneself from all enticement of the flesh and from evil passions." This is why so frequently in the Masses of the Lenten season one finds prayers in which the Church asks God that, while her members practice the fasting which is involved in forgoing certain foods, they will at the same time be given the strength necessary to avoid evil practices.

If penance is really understood, it is recognized as giving man the privilege of uniting his acts of sacrifice with the divine oblation which Christ offered on the cross, and which he continues to offer in the Mass. Penance assures those who practice it peace in this world, and eternal peace in heaven.

11

His Cross And Achievement

There is more to spiritual living than obtaining forgiveness for sin and atoning for it through penance. All this—forgiveness, penance, atonement—is the obverse side of the coin. It is the negative aspect of the Christian religion. The positive aspect is that which St. Peter had in mind when he said that, through Christ, we "become partakers of the divine nature." The cross not only atoned for the sins of the world, but also made possible for mankind a participation in the life of the Godhead.

Once we have received the divine life through grace, we can merit an increase of that life. We can also help others to share in the life of the Divinity. It is believed that St. Stephen's prayer at his martyrdom helped to obtain for St. Paul, not only the forgiveness of his sins, but the first graces needed for his justification. St. Monica appears to have done the same for her son, St. Augustine. This is the highest form of achievement, a participation in the achievement of the Son of God. And it is a form of achievement available to every member of the Church.

Ambition, if it is not prompted by unworthy motives, is praiseworthy. The normal person has a right to feel frustrated if he is accomplishing nothing worthwhile in life. The desire for achievement is actually a desire to imitate the Creator. This is one reason why we speak of great and unique achievements as *creations*.

But, if a person is going to be rational about it, he should desire to achieve something of real value, something that will help him and his fellowman, not something which will merely win him passing applause. St. Paul spoke of the perishable crown, the laurel wreath, for which the athletes of his day exerted such efforts and made such sacrifices. Nobody but a few scholars knows the name of a single record-breaking athlete acclaimed two thousand years ago by Greek or Roman crowds. But nearly every literate person on earth knows the name of St. Paul, and he has won the imperishable crown of eternal life, which he contrasted with the athlete's fading laurels.

The startling progress made in jet propulsion caused Pope Pius XII to declare that "man's efforts to conquer space . . . reveal in some manner the impulse urging man on to exceed himself." He saw behind such efforts a spiritual impulse which too many fail to recognize, an impulse in man "to grow morally and to find in his soul ever new resources of generosity and heroism."

The greatest achievement, the most generous and the most heroic, one that touches the life of every human being, dead or living, or yet to be born, appeared to most of those who witnessed it to be no achievement at all, but a complete defeat. But today, almost two thousand years after it was accomplished, eight hundred million people regard it as indeed the supreme achievement, the raising of the human race from sin to grace.

If God had called a conference of the wise ones of the world to suggest means of restoring the human race to grace, one wonders what recommendations would have been made. Surely nobody would have suggested that man be saved through a cross. But God has a way of turning the so-called wisdom of the world upside down, and the cross was the very means he used for this greatest of all achievements.

Mankind has a way of taking common things for granted. Every day the members of the Church make the beautiful gesture of signing themselves with the cross. They cover themselves with the cross. In this way they manifest their participation in the mystery of the cross. They identify themselves with the achievement of the crucified Christ.

Pope Pius XII, after stating that Christ did good by working miracles, but saved mankind by his suffering and death, went on to explain that we are given the tremendous privilege of participating in the achievement of the Son of God. In a special message to the sick, the Holy Father declared: "Jesus, by exhorting you to take up your cross and follow him, invited you by that very fact to cooperate with him in the work of redemption. As his heavenly Father invited him, so he invites you.... The Passion of Jesus shows you the fruitfulness of suffering for yourselves, for others, and for the world."

It is a mistake to measure success mainly by the amount of time gained on television or radio, by the number of conventions that are held, or by the amount of space covered with printer's ink. A single resigned cry from a soul in anguish may mean more in the way of real achievement than a thousand sermons by a popular preacher. St. Thérèse, whose stupendous achievement nobody can question, stated this in a letter to one of the foreign missionaries who had the privilege of corresponding with her. "It is, in truth," she wrote, "more through suffering and persecution, than by eloquent preaching, that Jesus wills to establish his kingdom in souls."

St. Thérèse linked achievement and the cross as end and means. She wrote in her *autobiography:* "If we want to attain an end we must employ the means, and Jesus made me understand that he would give me souls by means of the cross; the more crosses I met with, the more did my attraction to suffering increase."

She wrote in a similar vein to a missionary: "I do not desire to be delivered from the suffering of this life, because suffering united to love is the only thing which appears to me desirable in this valley of tears." Speaking in terms of the wisdom of God, these are the words of one of the wisest women of all time.

Usually implicit in the desire for achievement is the desire to influence others. It is not likely that many masterpieces of music or literature are lying hidden in desk drawers. If anybody wants really to influence others, if he wants to have the kind of influence that will extend to the ends of the earth, an influence that will reach perhaps into some obscure village in Africa or China, or into the heart of New York, he can have it. And he can exert it without moving a step from wherever he happens to be.

The Church being the Mystical Body of Christ, everything that a particular member does affects the whole body. This is why some very obscure person, lying neglected in a hospital ward and whose existence could not appear more useless and wasted to those who happen to pass by, may be winning the grace of conversion for some soul on the other side of the earth, a soul to whom a missionary may be inspired, through the transmuted power of consecrated suffering, to say a word which will penetrate like a steel blade, and leave that soul changed for all eternity.

This influence, like a wave that rises in the middle of the sea, can continue producing effects to unsuspected distances in time and space. Anybody, through his prayerful acceptance of the cross in his life, can influence souls unknown to him, and these in turn can influence others, and so on, right into eternity.

This is the idea behind St. Paul's statement that he made up in his own body those things which were lacking in the Passion of Christ. The tragedy in the world is not that there is suffering, but that so much suffering is wasted. And it is wasted because some of those who profess to believe in the cross rebel against the entrance of the cross into their own lives.

St. Peter wrote: "Unto this, indeed, you have been called, because Christ also has suffered for you, leaving you an example that you may follow in his steps." Christ's offering of himself was the great act of atonement. But this is only part of the mystery of the cross. The crosses of the members of his Church, united with the cross of Christ, are accepted by God as atonement for their sins and even the sins of others.

The greatness of the tragedy of the wasted cross is understood when it is recalled that there were three crosses on Calvary, and that one of them was eternally wasted. On the central cross, the Son of God wrought the world's supreme achievement, the salvation of mankind. Msgr. R. A. Knox fittingly translates the *consummatum est* of the crucified Christ, "it is achieved!" On one of the other crosses, the man who is now called the Good Thief achieved heroic sanctity in a matter of hours. On the third cross, his companion allowed Satan to cheat him of a similar achievement and lead him to eternal failure.

Sometimes people live in such obvious frustration that the consciousness of waste is overwhelming. They suffer from a withering boredom, constantly waiting for something to happen to break the gray monotony that appears to paralyze them. They are the personification of unfulfilled desires. They look out from eyes that are like the staring windows of a vacant house. The tragedy is that this kind of frustration and waste is unnecessary.

Pope Pius XII reminded those who "are afflicted with the burden of appearing to be useless" that this attitude is only outwardly true. "You are not useless. With your supernatural sorrow offered to Christ, you can protect so many souls, bring back to the right road so many who have erred, enlighten so many who are in doubt, and give serenity back to so many who grieve."

Words which are used in everyday speech are liable to lose their impact. And this is true of the word *cross* when used in reference to some trial one is asked to undergo. Christ first gave further meaning to the word when he said that anyone who failed to take up his cross daily could not be his disciple. True Christian insight prompted its continued use. Such spiritual insight makes the difference between useful and useless suffering.

The members of the Church are as truly one with Christ as the members of the human body are one with the head. Because of this oneness with him, the crosses of the members when offered with his cross have a consecrated character. Every disappointment, every temptation, every pain, every privation, willed or unwilled, every separation through death or distance is a cross that can be transmuted by the divine alchemy of his cross into the gold of God's forgiveness for some unknown person, into the gold of Christ's life surging through some soul who has never received it, or has deprived himself of it through sin, into the gold of that grace which is God's life in man during his earthly exile.

This is brought out in the words of a French priest who, after the invasion of France by the Nazis, accompanied French workmen conscripted for labor in Germany, not as a chaplain, but as a workman. Writing of the suffering of these men, Père Perrin said: "If you could translate the mass of their waiting and wretchedness, the cry of their hope, into gold coins, or light or harmony, it would transform the whole earth and shake it to its foundations, so that it would throb all over with glorious music that would rend the heart." Speaking of his own ordeal, and his being deprived of the opportunity to offer Mass, he wrote: "I had no bread to offer, but a day in prison was a precious offering in my hands."

World-shaking achievement, the kind that wins Nobel prizes and Pulitzer awards, is for the few. And some of these achievements will show blanks in the gold records of eternal life. Other achievements, such as rearing godly families, molding youth through religious education, caring for the fatherless, the infirm, and the aged, while little recognized by a materialistic generation, will loom large in eternity, but not everybody is in a position to mark up such achievement.

There is, however, one sort of achievement which is open to all. All men can take their crosses up the hill of Calvary: the illnesses, the separations, the disappointments, the frustrations, the temptations, the misunderstandings, the daily aggravations. There these crosses can be placed alongside the holy cross of the divine Redeemer. Surely, nobody can aspire to any more fruitful or lasting achievement than participation in the supreme achievement of the Son of God.

12

His Cross And Peace Of Soul

To attain peace is the greatest achievement of all. Peace means order, and order is the first and last law of this world and the other. Whether or not we achieve peace during our passage through time determines whether we will attain to the peace of eternal life.

Strange as it may appear, everybody on earth is seeking peace. Man is forever seeking rest for his restless mind and heart. Evidence for this is found in the various pursuits of mankind. The athlete, the actor, the scientist, the artist, the politician—all are seeking in their different professions rest for their ambitions.

Even the sinner is seeking peace, although the peace which he seeks in sin is a mirage conjured up by Satan. The avaricious seek to rest in their hoarded worldly goods, but their uncontrolled passion drives them to reach out greedy hands toward further possessions. The ambitious think to find rest in fame, although one writer who achieved it said that to have it is a purgatory, to want it is a hell. The sensual always hope to rest in their inordinate or illicit gratifications, but passion, like an untamed beast, drives them from excess to excess, and makes peace impossible for them.

St. Augustine says that peace is *the tranquility of order.* That peace is indeed the tranquility of order is seen vividly when we look into the minds and hearts of those who violently disturb the order of human lives. The thief, the adulterer, the murderer, the liar, the hatemonger, and the gossiper spread disorder in society because there is disorder in their hearts. The men who threaten mankind with the horrible disorder of war are men whose souls reflect the disorder of hell itself.

When it is said that peace is the tranquility of order, it must be kept in mind that order comes from God. The order which God put in the universe was shattered by sin. God willed to restore peace and order through the cross. As St. Paul expresses it, "it has pleased the Father that through him [Christ] he should reconcile to himself all things, *making peace through the blood of his cross.*" Moreover, those who have been received back to the embrace of the God of peace must strive all their lives to eliminate possible sources of disorder from their minds and hearts.

One source of disorder between God and man is rebellion against his will when his will takes the form of a cross. Unless one accepts his will as manifested through the events of life, sorrowful as well as joyful, one cannot be at harmony with God. Our divine Master left no doubt about this when he said: "If any man would come after me, let him deny himself and take up his cross and follow me" (Mark 8:34).

One of the joys of heaven will consist in understanding the perfect harmony between the divine and human natures in Christ, our Lord and our brother. It will then be seen that the human will of Jesus was so completely in harmony with the divine will that this harmony finally raised his human nature to the very throne of God. This harmony of the divine and human wills in Christ reached perfection through the cross. This is what St. Paul means when he says that "Jesus, who for the joy set before him, endured a cross, despising shame, and sits at the right hand of the throne of God."

Our Savior's human will was attuned perfectly to the will of his Father during the ordeal of his Crucifixion, because on the cross he continued in the perfect resignation to the will of his Father which he had demonstrated by his prayer in Gethsemane: "Yet not my will, but thine be done." Thus the God-Man not only used the cross as the instrument for restoring peace and harmony between God and man, but also as the pulpit from which he taught how that peace is to be preserved once it is achieved.

Christ is saying from the cross: "I have already taught you that, if you are to be pleasing to my Father, you must practice justice, and purity, and truthfulness, and kindness. I have shown you that these are the first steps toward union with God. Now, on the cross,

I am exemplifying that perfect union is possible only if you accept his will as manifested in the hard and difficult trials of earthly life. I am showing you what I meant when I said that if you wished to follow me in attaining complete harmony with God, you must embrace the cross."

At the Last Supper, our Lord prayed "that they may be one, even as we are . . . that all may be one, even as thou, Father, in me and I in thee; that they also may be one in us." This is the sublime prayer of the divine Redeemer for perfect unity between God and man, a unity which is perfected through man's acceptance of the trials that are intended to purify and ripen him. John Donne expressed a great deal in a few words when he wrote: "No man hath affliction enough that is not matured and ripened by it, and made fit for God by that affliction."

Every human life may be compared to a tapestry that God himself is weaving for the adornment of his eternal mansions. A tapestry would have no beauty or harmony if there were no shades to heighten the bright parts of the design. The shades are the trials of earthly life. If trials cease, a man should wonder whether, through his lack of resignation, he has not stayed God's hand in completing his design in his soul.

Nothing could be clearer from holy Scripture than that man's will is brought into harmony with God's will through earthly trials. The Archangel Raphael said to Tobit: "And because you were acceptable to God, it was necessary that temptation should prove you." Again, God said to the bishop of Laodicea: "As for me, those whom I love I rebuke and chastise."

Human nature instinctively recoils from suffering. And yet, the Acts of the Apostles and the Epistles show the Apostles actually exulting in opportunities to participate in the Passion and cross of Christ. They did so because they realized that, through their crosses, they were being perfected for union with their crucified Lord. And this, they well knew, meant union with God.

The Acts state that after the Apostles had been scourged by the Jewish Sanhedrin, they departed "*rejoicing* that they had been counted *worthy to suffer* disgrace for the name of Jesus." The Epistles echo and reecho the *"rejoice and exult"* attitude which Christ tells his followers to have "when men reproach you, and persecute you, and, speaking falsely, say all manner of evil against you."

St. Peter wrote to the first members of the Church: "Beloved, do not be startled at the trial by fire that is taking place among you *to prove you,* as if something strange were happening to you; *but insofar as you are partakers of the suffering of Christ, rejoice* that you may also rejoice with exultation in the revelation of his glory." St. Paul reminds the Romans that "we *exult in tribulations.*" St. James opens his Epistle on the same note: *"Count it all joy, my brethren, when you meet various trials"* (Jas. 1:2).

The Church carries this spirit of exultation in participation in the Passion into her liturgy. On the Feast of St. Andrew, who was crucified, the Church has the Apostle exclaiming: "Hail, precious cross; receive the disciple of him who hung upon thee, even Christ, my Master." The same theme is found in other parts of the liturgy. On the feast of St. Marcellus in the old calendar, the collect of the Mass and Office reads: "Mercifully hear, we beseech thee, O Lord, the prayer of thy people, that we who *rejoice* in the martyrdom of the blessed Marcellus, thy martyr and pope, may be aided by his merits." And in the introit of the Mass of St. Agatha, the Church has us exclaim: "Let us all *rejoice* in the Lord, *celebrating a festival* in honor of the blessed Agatha, *at whose passion the angels rejoice* and give praise to the Son of God."

Such unanimity in finding joy in crosses indicates one source of doctrine. These men and women, of various backgrounds and temperaments, learned the one and only philosophy taught by their divine Master from the cross. There is here the flowering of the one faith, the working of the one Spirit, who continues to unfold in the Church the wisdom of the cross.

The key to this Christian paradox of finding joy and peace through suffering is given in that phrase in the Acts, "rejoicing that they had been *counted worthy to suffer.*" Counted worthy to suffer! This is one of the greatest of Christian mysteries which can be understood only by those who have pondered and lived it.

Fr. Dominic Barberi, the Passionist who received Cardinal

Newman into the Church, explained the paradox to a correspondent when he wrote: "You ask my blessing, and I ask God to bless you. But, madam, the most generous blessings of God are crosses, and patience to bear them. The souls most acceptable to his majesty have always been laden with crosses."

That God's most generous blessings are crosses was discovered by the wife of Léon Bloy. She expressed this in a striking passage: "One day, reminding Jesus of our extreme poverty, I said to him, 'Open thy hand, Lord, and give us what it contains.' Jesus opened his hand, and I saw that it was pierced." St. Paul of the Cross had the same idea in mind when he wrote to a sick woman: "His divine majesty wishes to make you a portrait of Jesus crucified." John Donne expressed it in another way:

> "When that cross ungrudged unto you sticks,
> Then you are to yourself a crucifixe."

In a beautiful tribute to St. Jane Frances de Chantal, St. Francis de Sales compares trials accepted from the hand of God to musical harmony. He says of St. Jane Frances, who for forty years sustained heroic sacrifices for Christ: "She played wondrous music but, like one deaf, heard nothing of the melody." The same note is found in lines by Joyce Kilmer:

> "They shall not live who have not tasted death;
> They only sing who are struck dumb by God."

The Jewish philosopher and convert, St. Edith Stein, who as Sr. Teresa Benedicta of the Cross, Discalced Carmelite, was to suffer death in a Nazi gas chamber, admirably exemplified this union of the cross and harmonious living. A Jewish businessman who met her as a prisoner in a German concentration camp in Holland before she was brought back to Germany for martyrdom, wrote: "Among the prisoners . . . Sr. Benedicta stood out because of her calmness and composure. The distress in the barracks, and the stir caused by new arrivals, were indescribable. Sr. Benedicta was just like an angel, going around among the women, comforting them, helping them, calming them." It is hardly surprising that she wrote to her prioress at this time: "One can only learn a knowledge of the cross if one feels the cross in one's own person."

One of the most striking confirmations that spiritual harmony is achieved through peaceful acceptance of crosses is the Godlike harmony radiated by those who accept great trials with great resignation. A concrete illustration of this can be found in any hospital.

From one patient who rebels against trial emanates an air of disturbance. The air is charged. The sense of disturbance is tangible. From another patient, suffering perhaps more than the other, but accepting his cross as "the shade of his hand outstretched caressingly," emanates an air of peace. The peace is also tangible. Everybody around feels refreshed and uplifted by it.

Cardinal Newman recalled that "in the cross we shall first find sorrow, but in a while peace and comfort will rise out of that sorrow." "All this sorrow," he says, "will only issue, nay, will be undergone in happiness greater than the enjoyment which the world gives." He was echoing the words of Christ: "You shall be sorrowful, but your sorrow shall be turned to joy . . . you therefore have sorrow now; but I will see you again, and your heart shall rejoice, and your joy no one shall take from you."

When winter comes, it is endured more easily because spring will follow, and the cold, frost, and snow of winter will be no more. So it is with crosses. They are to be embraced because they will be followed in time and eternity by the peace of the Prince of Peace. One learns to accept them in the spirit of him "who for the joy set before him endured a cross." His cross shows that suffering is truly the path to peace.

One can acquire this attitude only if one prays for it. One should ask God for the grace to do and accept his will perfectly. This petition comprehends every grace, including the greatest peace in this life and eternal peace in the next. Such was St. Paul's prayer for the Hebrews: "May the God of peace . . . fit you with every good thing to do his will."

13

His Cross And Human Relations

Any consideration of peace in general naturally leads to a consideration of that particular peace which is associated with fraternal love. Since peace is the tranquility of order, if one's relations with others are in good order, one must be at peace with one's fellowman. It is hardly surprising that the Church often links the terms, unity and peace, in the liturgy. In the prayer over the gifts of the Mass of Corpus Christi, the Church recalls that Christ gave men the Holy Eucharist to unite in peace man with man, and all men with God:

> "We beseech thee, O Lord, graciously grant to
> thy Church the gifts of unity and peace, which
> are mystically signified by the gifts we offer.
> Through Christ our Lord."

The resplendent love of Christianity shines all the more brilliantly when placed against the satanic hate of Communism. If one places the love of the Christian saints against the malice of the leaders of world Communism, one understands what Christ meant when he said that by their fruits you shall know them.

Compare the writings of a St. Francis de Sales, expositor of the doctrine of love, with the writings of a Karl Marx, expositor of hate. Compare the constructive benevolence of a St. Teresa of Avila with the destructive malevolence of a Spanish Loyalist La Pasionaria. Compare the justice, mercy, and peace of a St. Pius X with the injustice, mercilessness, and violence of a Stalin.

There are now two great world symbols, and both of these are crosses. One represents love, the other represents hate. One is the divine cross of Christ, whose arms are outstretched to embrace all mankind. The other is the twisted cross of the hammer and sickle, which is poised to cut down or bludgeon into submission all who refuse to exalt it.

The battle that goes on constantly in this world is the earthly counterpart of the battle that went on in heaven between Michael and Lucifer. Stalin was just confusing the issue when he asked Churchill during World War II how many divisions the Pope had. The battle is not so much for populations and territories as it is for the minds of men. The real issue is whether men's minds will be won over to love or to hatred.

What is involved is the whole area of divine and human love. Love and hate are far from being mathematical things. But nothing prevents one from considering them in a mathematical way for the sake of clarity. If hate grows, love must recede. If love increases, hate must be pushed back.

God's love, which was manifested with such munificence on the cross, has not reached more human hearts because many of those who outwardly honor the cross fail to exalt it through imitation of the love which it represents. It is again the question of how deeply the cross is pondered by those who every day sign themselves with the cross, who trace the cross over their minds, lips, and hearts, who wear the cross on their persons, who place it on the walls of their homes.

God is love, as St. John says, and love must, by its nature, give of itself. Love is like those liquids whose property is to expand and overflow. It was through love that God created all things, visible and invisible. It was through love that he created the world. It was through love that he made man. But creation cost God nothing. He had merely to will it, and the world and man and all created things came into existence.

It seems almost that God envied man his ability to prove his love through sacrifice. God, as God, could not sacrifice himself. As God made man, however, Christ could suffer. He could endure for all mankind the concentrated agony of what one writer acquainted with crucifixion called the most savage of torments. He could redeem the creatures of his hand by offering himself to a form of execution so savage and inhuman that it was forbidden to inflict such a death on any citizen of the Roman Empire.

The poet once wrote: "Not what we give but what we share, the gift without the giver is bare." Blood is life, and the Son of God literally poured out his life through head and hands and feet and side. The gift on the cross was nothing less than the life of the giver. If ever a giver gave himself with his gift, it was Christ on Calvary.

This supreme giver issued a challenge to those who would accept his teaching. What he issued in fact was a commandment, but it still constitutes a challenge. He said: "This is my commandment, that you love one another as I have loved you" (John 15:12). Before he came, the commandment was to love others as one loves oneself. Now the commandment is to love others to the point of heroism, in imitation of the most heroic love that the world has ever seen, or will ever see.

Christ left no doubt about what he meant when he commanded a love like his own. For it was immediately after he had given this command that he said: "Greater love has no man than this, that a man lay down his life for his friends" (John 15:13). St. Paul was recalling this essential teaching of the divine Savior when he said that those who follow him are called to be "imitators of God and walk in love, as Christ loved us and delivered himself up for us."

Our Lord emphasized that all the world would be able to distinguish his followers by the way in which they imitated his heroic love. He thus implied that those who lack this love for their fellowman are his followers in name only. It will not be the number of candles a person has lighted, nor the number of shrines that he has visited, nor the number of rosaries that he has said, that will count most when he goes before Christ for his reckoning. It will be principally the love that he has shown to others.

In his description of the Judgment, Christ mentions only this virtue of love. Men will be judged on all the other virtues, but the Master gives them to understand that there will be no hope for anyone who has failed to reach out his hand to a homeless, hungry, lonely, sick, or otherwise needy brother. William Langland expressed it all very well when he said that chastity without charity will be chained in hell.

Love must be extended first to those with whom one lives and associates. There are people who display exuberant good-fellowship toward outsiders but show anything but love and affection for their own. There are others who restrict their love to their families and a small circle of friends but are cold to anybody outside the circle. It has been well said that a man loves Christ as much as he loves the person he loves least. The person an individual loves least is the person he is least willing to assist. It can be further said that if there is any person on earth who is excluded from one's love, one does not love Christ at all.

There are evidently those who think that this commandment to love others to the point of sacrifice can be left to heroic groups within the Church. They seem to feel that they can leave a self-sacrificing love of others to the Little Sisters of the Poor, who pour our their sacrificial love on thousands of the aged poor. Or that they can leave the practical love of others to the Sisters of the Good Shepherd, who give themselves to the thousands of confused young women whom they receive into their houses. Or that the Church will have fulfilled its office of bringing Christ's love to mankind if the priests, brothers, and sisters who teach the ignorant, nurse the sick, and care for the orphaned will only continue their heroic work.

But the Church needs more than the specialists in love. She needs more than the men and women who are pouring out their lives for their fellowman in prayer and penance in the cloister. She needs more than the Nardins, the Legionaries of Mary, the Parish Visitors, the men of St. Vincent de Paul, the conductors of Friendship House and Houses of Hospitality.

The Church needs more than these self-sacrificing men and women if she is to spread the fire that Christ said he came to cast upon earth. The Church needs a great awakening to the need of a personal carrying out of our Lord's commandment of love, a personal imitation of the heroic love which he demonstrated on the cross.

The mistake is sometimes made of thinking of the Church as a super Catholic Charities office. This leads to one's becoming convinced that it is enough if one contributes a mite to some charity or if one helps toward the construction of some church building. The material apparatus that the Church uses could disappear—the church buildings, the schools, the hospitals, the monasteries, and the convents. If this were to happen, the Church would still exist, because the Church is not made up of buildings, but of people. All Catholics united with Christ form the Church. Nobody, therefore, can reasonably say: The Church will take care of loving people. A person who speaks in this way sounds as though he looks on the Church as apart from himself. In the Church particularly is it true that no man is an island to himself.

The golden rule is as golden as ever, but those to whom it was given have perhaps allowed it to become tarnished through lack of use. Christ was not talking to the few when he said: "Therefore, all that you wish men to do to you, even so do you also to them." Every man knows what he wants from others—generosity when he is in need, sympathy when he is in trouble, forgiveness when he has offended. He wants others to be thoughtful, considerate, friendly, cheerful. Well, they want him also to manifest these qualities. And he who claims to follow him who gave his life on the cross through love must be first in manifesting them.

14

His Cross And Length Of Life

Few questions interest man more than how long he will live. One of the first questions asked when somebody dies is: How old was he? Newspaper obituaries usually mention the age of the deceased in the first paragraph: "William Q. White died at a hospital in Old New York today after a short illness. His age was 77." "Mary N. London, 35, died at her home yesterday after an illness of two years." The curiosity that people have regarding the ages of friends or persons of prominence is heightened when their death is announced.

It is interesting to analyze this curiosity. The explanation appears to be rather simple. People want to know how many years the deceased was allowed to spend in this world. If he was given more than sixty or seventy years, the reaction is liable to be: He was blessed to have lived more than threescore years. If he was given less than thirty or forty, the comment is almost sure to be: How tragic!

A friend tells a man how well be looks, and the friend receives a rewarding smile. The implication is that a healthy appearance justifies one in looking forward to many years of healthy and happy living. A physician tells a patient that he is in fine condition, and the patient leaves the doctor's office as though he has just been handed a thousand dollars.

One of the achievements of our era has been the prolongation of human life. Magazines and newspapers are filled with statistics showing how much longer people live today than they did fifty years ago. Research in processes of rejuvenation is carried on with ever-growing intensity. But the cross shows that in the book of

God's eternal wisdom, a term like life expectancy is not so important as it is sometimes represented.

It was not by chance that Christ died at the age he did. With God, nothing happens by chance. Since God became man, with the intention of dying, he had to set a limit to the days and years that he would spend on earth. Because he was God, he could have willed to die after having lived in this world for a hundred years, or a thousand, or as long as he chose.

If somebody dies in his thirties, there is a temptation to think that somehow he has been cheated. But Christ died in his middle thirties. It is doubtful that even his closest followers very often advert to the fact that our Savior was so young when he gave his life on the cross. One reason for this might be that in many representations of him on the cross, he could be any age, from thirty to sixty.

In heaven, where all mysteries will be explained, it will likely be discovered that there was some deeply hidden reason for his dying at that particular age. Apart from such a hidden purpose, Christ is demonstrating by his early death that with God the important thing will not be the length of one's life span, but in what way one will have spent the years, long or short, that God sees fit to give.

This whole idea of the relative unimportance of the amount of time that a person spends on earth is strikingly confirmed in the saints. Whether they died in old age, in middle age, or in youth, they understood what their crucified young Master was teaching them in this regard. St. Thérèse summed up the attitude of all of them when she said that, if she were given a choice of long or short life, she would not choose.

The spread between the ages of different saints is very great. St. Maria Goretti, for instance, gave her life in defense of her chastity after a little more than a decade in this world. The lives of St. Paul of the Cross and St. Alphonsus spanned more than eight and nine decades, respectively. Is it fanciful to suppose that God gave St. Alphonsus ninety-one years because he had made a vow not to waste time? Ordinarily, however, one does not dwell on the fact that there was a difference in age of eighty years between such saints as Maria Goretti and Alphonsus Liguori, but that they both achieved sanctity. Various ages of the saints are noted to show that, when it comes to holiness, age is unimportant.

The boy martyr of the third century, St. Venantius, and the boy confessor of the twentieth, St. Dominic Savio, meet above the centuries, and agree that their time on earth, both having died at the age of fifteen, was long enough to learn and put into practice the wisdom taught by their young Savior from the cross.

During the past century, a number of saints completed the work of their sanctification in their twenties. Among them are the young Passionist, St. Gabriel; the young Carmelite, St. Thérèse; and the young laywoman, St. Gemma, all of whom died at the age of twenty-four. They all underscore the truth of the declaration of the writer of the Book of Wisdom: "Being perfect in a short space, *he fulfilled a long time.*"

What could better illustrate the relative unimportance of age than the impact of the young heroine, St. Thérèse, on the world. Some are misled by the oversweet statues and pictures of her that are so common. They see the roses, but not the crucifix, which she is represented as carrying in her arms. They thus miss the essential meaning of her greatness. The roses, which are symbolic of the shower of graces and favors which she has been sending from heaven ever since her death, would not be there if she had not understood and lived the doctrine of the cross. It was her understanding of the wisdom of the cross that prompted her to write that "age is nothing in the sight of God."

If further illustration is desired regarding the possibility of accomplishing a great deal in a short time, one can consider two saints who, like our Lord, died in their thirties. St. Catherine of Siena showed not only that sanctity can be achieved in a few decades, but that very great external work can be brought to completion in a few years. In her thirty-three years, she not only reached the highest union with God possible on earth, but composed treatises which are considered mines of spiritual knowledge, gave advice to ecclesiastical and temporal rulers, and surrounded herself with disciples whom she guided to great spiritual heights.

It is more than seven centuries since St. Anthony of Padua died at the age of thirty-five, after only ten years in the priesthood. Thirty-five is only half the life expectancy of men in the United States today. But the three and a half decades of this man were so fruitful that, in the year 1946, the Vicar of Christ and the minister general of the Franciscan order, of which St. Anthony was a member, seemed to be trying to outdo each other in his praise.

While considering that such young men and women have had such a powerful effect on the whole Church for the duration of time, we should not lose sight of the source of their power, the cross of their young Savior. That the cross was the cause and inspiration of the fruitfulness of their few years on earth is highlighted by certain facts in their lives. St. Catherine's union with our Lord in his Passion was so great that she received the marks of his wounds in her body. And only in the cross could St. Anthony have found the strength, not only to accept death at the height of a most successful preaching career, but to meet it joyfully singing his favorite hymn to our Lady.

Saints who died in their forties confirm the importance of the idea that length of life is not essential. St. Francis of Assisi, whose order has given the Church hundreds of saints, and whose friars even now, seven centuries after his death, number more than 35,000, not to mention the thousands of nuns who claim him as their spiritual father, lived only forty-four years. He also showed that the cross was his supreme inspiration by receiving the stigmata. St. Francis Xavier, whose influence on India and Japan is still being felt, was forty-six at his death. St. Thomas Aquinas, who wrote volume after volume of profound philosophy and sublime theology, was forty-nine when he died.

Other saints were given longer lives. St. Dominic, St. Thomas More, and St. Francis de Sales were in their fifties when death came. St. Benedict, St. Bernard, and St. Teresa of Avila were in their sixties. St. Augustine, St. John Vianney, and St. John Bosco died in their seventies. St. Vincent de Paul, St. Paul of the Cross, and St. Philip Neri reached their eighties. St. Alphonsus lived into his nineties. St. Anthony, the first abbot and founder of monasticism, and St. Paul, the first hermit, were both more than a hundred when they died.

Centuries before the coming of Christ, God inspired the author of the Book of Ecclesiastes to write: "Better is a child that is poor and wise, than a king that is old and foolish." And the Book of Wisdom says that "venerable old age is not that of a long time, nor counted by the number of years."

But it remained for Christ, the Incarnate Wisdom of God, to spell out this truth with that unique eloquence which goes with example. In the cross, that book of wisdom which he alone could properly write, he proclaims that the important thing with God is not the quantity of our days on earth, but their quality.

Time is, indeed, of the essence, but not in the sense that one needs a lot of it. It is of the essence in the sense that it is the raw material out of which one's eternity is to be fashioned. It is true that a man can *kill* time, but he should not deceive himself into believing that this will not injure him in eternity. Divine wisdom is telling men, by the use he made of the thirty-three years which he climaxed on the cross, not to be concerned whether their years be few or many, but to be very much concerned about the way in which they use the years that God wills to give them.

15

His Cross And Its Anticipation

There is an aspect of the cross to which perhaps we do not give sufficient attention. This is the fact that our Lord suffered his Passion by anticipation all his earthly life. St. Margaret Mary says our Savior revealed to her that from the first moment of his Incarnation the torments of his Passion had been present to him. "From the first moment," she writes, "the cross, as it were, had been planted in his Heart."

Anticipation of some inevitable trial frequently magnifies the suffering that is bound to accompany it. There is a proneness in many people to expect the worst. But in the case of our Lord, the worst was actually inevitable once he had come into the world in fulfillment of the prophecy of the psalmist: "Burnt offering and sin offering thou didst not require: then said I, Behold I come." There was no question of Christ's conjuring up sufferings that might not materialize. He simply knew, through his divine foreknowledge, every detail of the incredible sufferings that awaited him. His Passion thus hung like a pall over all his days.

Mental suffering is often much harder to bear than physical pain. Sometimes a person who is merely threatened with a painful disease will experience such mental distress that he will, to his eternal loss, seek release through self-inflicted death. Our Redeemer had to bear the mental anguish of looking forward, not only to sufferings of indescribable intensity, but to sufferings which would be unique because of the Person who would endure them.

The Old Testament prophets could foretell the sufferings of the coming Messiah only because they were given, by the Holy Spirit, some obscure knowledge of these sufferings. Christ knew them, not obscurely, but in their full reality. Many prophetic references to the longed-for Savior were filled with undertones of his sufferings. The risen Christ was to take the two disciples on the road to Emmaus through a review of the Scriptures to pinpoint the prophecies concerning his Passion. "And beginning with Moses and all the prophets, he interpreted to them in all the Scriptures the things concerning himself" (Luke 24:27). The prophecies he recalled must have referred mainly to his Passion, for he concluded: "Was it not necessary that the Christ should suffer these things and enter into his glory?" (Luke 24:26).

Christ knew far better than Isaiah the meaning of the latter's prophecy concerning the Redeemer: "Despised and rejected by men; a man of sorrows, and acquainted with grief; and as one from whom men hide their faces . . . we esteemed him stricken, smitten by God, and afflicted" (Is. 53:3–4). Jesus not only lived with these words all his life on earth, but saw with his divine intelligence that their fulfillment would make them look like an understatement.

We find implicit references to his sufferings also in the declarations that were made concerning him immediately before his entrance into the world, and at the time of it. One example is the message of the angel who appeared to Joseph in a dream, telling him about the approaching Virgin Birth. The angel commanded him to call the Son who was to be born to Mary *Jesus*, which means Savior, because, as the messenger explained, "he shall save his people from their sins." Becoming Savior meant, according to Isaiah, being wounded for our iniquities and bruised for our sins.

Even on that most joyful night, when the skies were filled with a heavenly radiance and the song of angelic choirs, the angel who addressed the shepherds referred to the Savior as *Christ*, thus giving prophetic intimation of the sacrifice that he would offer. The title *Christ* is fraught with the concept of suffering. The title means the *Anointed One*. Christ is anointed as *Priest*, as the great High Priest. A priest's office is to offer sacrifice. Jesus was anointed as Priest from the moment of his Incarnation for the bloody sacrificial offering which he would make of himself on the cross.

One of the most joyous incidents in the Gospels is the Presentation of our Lord in the Temple. Receiving the infant

Christ into his arms, the aged Simeon ecstatically thanked God for fulfilling his promise that Simeon would not die without seeing the Redeemer. But even in the midst of his unutterable joy, he was inspired to prophesy regarding our Lord's Passion, saying that the Child was a sign which would be contradicted. That this contradiction would involve great suffering was indicated when Simeon turned to Mary and added that her heart would be pierced by a sword.

Similar prophetic intimations of the Passion are found in John the Baptist's references to our Lord. One day Jesus approached as John was preaching. John interrupted his sermon, pointed to Christ, and exclaimed: "Behold the Lamb of God, who takes away the sins of the world!" The next day, when John was standing with two of his disciples, our Lord again approached. And again the Baptist said: "Behold the Lamb of God!" The two disciples heard him speak, and they followed Jesus. On these two occasions, John came right to the point. Here was the Savior, but he called him *Lamb of God.* Among the Hebrews, the lamb carried connotations of sacrifice, for it was frequently used in the Temple sacrifices. What Israelite could forget that the blood of the paschal lamb saved his forefathers from the death visited on the firstborn of the Egyptians?

The detailed knowledge that our Redeemer had of his approaching suffering could not have been more clearly revealed than it was in his statement preparing his Apostles for the "scandal" of his Passion. "Behold we are going up to Jerusalem," he said, "and all things that have been written through the prophets concerning the Son of Man will be accomplished. For he will be delivered to the Gentiles, and will be mocked and scourged and spit upon; and after they have scourged him, they will put him to death." At the Last Supper, he spoke to the Apostles about the blood which he was about to shed for them and the world for the forgiveness of sins.

What the anticipation of his Passion meant to our Lord can be understood only if one realizes that the intensity of the sufferings of the divine Redeemer can hardly be exaggerated. Cicero said that crucifixion was the cruelest and blackest of torments. In the case of the Savior, there preceded the actual Crucifixion all those torments which, together with the Crucifixion, we call the sacred Passion.

The accumulation of these preceding sufferings was so grievous that Pilate used them to appeal to any human feeling that might be found in the cruel hearts of our Lord's enemies. This attempt reached its climax in the dramatic cry of the Roman governor as he presented the scourged and thorn-crowned Christ to the people: "Behold the man!"

No human mind can fathom the cosmic sadness and desolation that swept over the soul of Jesus in Gethsemane. There are depths of mental torment never plumbed by even the saints in what we have come to call the Agony in the Garden. St. Mark gives a hint of that sea of agony in his poignant statement: "And he began to feel dread and to be exceedingly troubled."

In considering the scourging, it must be borne in mind that it was done according to the Roman method, which set no limit to the number of strokes of the lash. The Jewish law forbade going beyond forty, "lest thy brother depart shamefully torn before thine eyes." The pressing down of the thorny crown was a refinement of cruelty that could have been inspired only by hell. As though all this were not enough, they jostled him, struck him, and spat in his sacred face.

We are appalled that one who has endured so much should be laden with his own cross and forced to carry it along the narrow route to Calvary. His persecutors were so fearful that what he had already suffered might prevent their enjoying the sadistic satisfaction of seeing him nailed to the cross that they forced Simon of Cyrene to assist him.

Anyone who has meditated on the Crucifixion of our divine Savior must be overwhelmed with the ghastly agonies that he endured. We cannot begin to realize the paroxysms of pain caused by the squared nails that had been driven into his hands and feet. Think of the impossibility of moving his body to get relief, the cramping of the muscles, the dreadful feeling of suffocation, the burning thirst. Consider the terrifying feeling of being abandoned by his Father, which caused him to give utterance to that cry of desolation: "My God, my God, why hast thou forsaken me?"

It may well be doubted that such an intensity of agony has ever been crowded into such a short space of time. Moreover, these tortures were harder for Christ to bear because his was a perfect body. This meant that his senses were more acute, including the sense of touch. The more sensitive the body, the more it feels pain. St. Thomas calls attention to the fact that, because of the perfect constitution of our Lord's body, death could not enter unless preceded by the most tremendous and dreadful of sufferings.

Nor can we overlook the mental anguish, which was all the greater because of the majesty of the Person. The derision, ridicule, and blasphemy marking the Crucifixion were all hurled against one who was Christ, the Son of the living God.

This is what Christ had to face from the moment of his Incarnation. We use the sword of Damocles as a symbol of the terror that can be experienced by the mere threat of suffering and death. But evidently the sword, which was reported to have been suspended by a hair over Damocles' head by order of the king of Syracuse, was never permitted to fall. The cross, which hung over our Lord all his days, was no mere threat. He knew from the beginning that he would be nailed to it, to hang from it in agony until he was dead. The long shadow of the cross fell back over the whole thirty-three years he willed to spend in this world. This should be a source of great strength and inspiration particularly for those whose suffering is of long duration.

16

His Cross And Victory

In the last analysis, what man seeks is victory in a variety of forms. He seeks victory over disease, ignorance, and a host of other enemies. For a Christian, all other victories are hollow, unless they lead to reigning victoriously with Christ in heaven.

It is strange that the most definitive triumph in man's history should have appeared to those who witnessed it as an utter defeat. Almost everything on Calvary seemed to spell failure for him who had been put to death so ignominiously. The tortured body of Christ was hanging limply from the cross, his head bowed in death. His enemies were taking a last, satisfied look at his lifeless figure, and were congratulating each other on what appeared to be their complete victory. His Apostles, acting like a small band of defeatists, were hiding behind the barred doors of the Cenacle.

The apparent defeat of Jesus looked so final that it kept the disciples plunged in gloom into the third day. Even the first reports of the empty tomb did not help to lift the pall which enshrouded them. After the reception of that news, two of the disciples did not think it worthwhile to remain in Jerusalem to await possibly hopeful developments. They started to walk to Emmaus, a village about eight miles from Jerusalem. Their depression was so obvious that, when the risen Christ joined them under the guise of a stranger who happened to be going the same way, he asked them what made them so sad.

Failing to recognize the Savior, they expressed surprise that he should be unaware of the great events which had so stirred Jerusalem during the past few days. They then explained that their melancholy was due to the Crucifixion of Jesus, "who was a prophet," they said, "mighty in deed and word before God and all the people" (Luke 24:19). Finally, they laid bare their total sense of defeat by blurting out in desperation: "We had hoped that he was the one to redeem Israel" (Luke 24:21). Their whole tone and bearing indicated that they were convinced that the Crucifixion had dashed this hope cruelly and completely.

Christ, still concealing his identity, chided them for their failure to understand what the Scriptures had foretold of his Passion. He took them back through the Old Testament, pointing out the numerous prophecies concerning the great sufferings of the long-awaited Messiah. When he had finished, he challenged their attitude toward the cross with the question: "Was it not necessary that the Christ should suffer these things and enter into his glory?" (Luke 24:26).

In speechless wonder, they finally recognized him "in the breaking of the bread." And when he had disappeared, they spoke of how their hearts had burned within them as he had interpreted the prophecies regarding his Passion. Never have two men risen so suddenly from dejection to exultation. They now saw that what they had considered cause for discouragement was really cause for elation. The cross, they now understood with divine clarity, instead of being a defeat, was a resounding victory.

The transformation of the Apostles from timid, fearful men into men of absolute confidence was completed with the coming of the Holy Spirit on Pentecost. Once they had received the Spirit, they left the Cenacle with the air of men who could not have been more convinced that victory was on their side. St. Peter, preaching in the name of all, disclosed the source of their confidence by recounting the events of Good Friday.

Naturally, St. Peter spoke of the Resurrection of Christ, but he emphasized that Christ's rising from the dead was a victorious result of his having given himself over to the death of the cross. "Therefore," he told his thousands of listeners, "let all the house of Israel know most assuredly that God has made both Lord and Christ, this Jesus whom you crucified." The first Vicar of Christ was losing no time in raising the cross as the victorious standard of the Church.

Jesus had told the Apostles that when the Holy Spirit came, he would recall to their minds everything that he himself had said to them. Now the Spirit made them understand why, during his public ministry, our Lord had made so many references to his Crucifixion and death. Now they saw why he had spoken of his death as a baptism, and why he had said that he was distressed until this baptism should be accomplished. Now it was clear to them that he had been awaiting his Crucifixion as an athlete who is confident of winning eagerly awaits the contest which will be the occasion of his triumph.

They also understood that strange conversation which Christ had held with Moses and Elijah during his Transfiguration, the one occasion before his Passion when he had allowed his divinity to shine resplendently. These two great figures of the Old Testament had talked with Jesus about his approaching death, a seemingly somber subject to discuss in such a triumphant setting. Now it was evident that nothing could have been more appropriate, for his death was not only to be a triumph, but a triumph of stupendous proportions.

The dimensions of the victory which Christ won through his cross are seen when we consider that the cross sundered the shackles with which sin had fettered mankind. The cross closed the gates of hell, and swung open the gates of heaven, for all who will to share in Christ's victory by accepting the redemption which he holds out to them. The cross caused the human nature which Christ had assumed to be raised to the right hand of the throne of God.

Victory is defined as the overcoming of an enemy, or of any difficulty. Victory follows combat. The victory of Christ can be shared only if men war against any disbelief or ignorance in their minds, and any moral evil in their wills. The arms that must be used to achieve victory in the battle of life are revealed with stark simplicity by St. Paul when he says that the Church preaches "a crucified Christ . . . the power of God and the wisdom of God." The implication in these words is that men will win in the warfare of earthly life if the wisdom which Christ taught from the cross saturates their minds, and if the power which he won through his cross invigorates their wills.

The world has never lacked men who have sought victory over the human mind by establishing schools of thought. Few men, however, have been in a better position than St. Paul to work out a system of thought and establish a school of philosophy, for he was an intellectual genius as well as a spiritual one. But the purpose of a system of thought should be the conquering of ignorance and the triumph of truth. And St. Paul realized that nothing could have been more futile and impertinent than engaging in a purely human search for truth and wisdom once the Incarnate Wisdom of God had given a compendium of wisdom and truth through his cross.

St. Paul was concerned "lest the cross of Christ be made void," if he were so foolish as to teach "with the wisdom of words." He is speaking here ironically of human wisdom when it is unguided by the wisdom of the cross. He became so convinced of the towering futility of any so-called wisdom that contradicted or obscured the wisdom of the cross that he wrote with impressive finality that "I determined not *to know anything* among you, except Jesus Christ and *Him Crucified.*" The great Apostle could not have made it clearer that man's mind will be victorious over its darkness only if it is flooded with the light that streams from the cross.

The spiritual victory of the Church has always been proportionate to her application of the wisdom of the cross. Whenever her members have depended on worldly wisdom, they have failed spiritually. When they have acted on the wisdom of the cross, they have marked up one victory after another. This is vividly illustrated in the saints, who have chosen poverty rather than riches, humiliation rather than honor, self-denial rather than pleasure, death rather than a life characterized by betrayal of God and his truth. None but unbelievers would question the victory that the saints have achieved through their application of the wisdom of the cross. Their triumph is decisive and eternal.

If the evil forces of injustice and hate have had a series of passing victories, it has been because the cross has been ignored as the symbol of divine wisdom, justice, and love. The German poet Heinrich Heine predicted in the last century that when the restraining influence of the cross was removed, the hammer of Thor, the pagan god of thunder, would smash the Gothic cathedrals, monuments to the moral power of the cross. The hammer of Thor has taken the shape in our time of the swastika and the hammer and sickle.

These diabolical crosses have engaged in a duel with the cross of the Son of God. The swastika is buried in the dust with the demagogue who tried to use it to supplant the cross of Christ. The cross of the hammer and sickle has been shaken, and it, too, in God's time, will perish in permanent defeat with its godless promoters.

When nations have learned wisdom the hard way, the cross always emerges in victory after the most vicious attacks upon it. The perennial triumph of the cross was symbolized by the restoration, a decade after World War II, of the great Cologne cathedral, which had been smashed because men had forgotten the cross of the Savior. The triumph of the cross was also symbolized by the emergence from imprisonment, in Hungary and in Poland, of two princes of the Church, whose cardinalatial red is a token of "the blood of his cross."

Napoleon, who won many military victories but ended in defeat, learned finally during his exile on the island of St. Helena that worldly victories were as so much smoke when compared with the eternal triumph of the cross of Christ. Napoleon wrote: "Christ expected success through his death on the cross. Could this be man's invention? I do not see any army, but some mysterious energizing power, and a few men scattered here and there in all quarters of the globe, with no other rallying point except a common faith in the mystery of the cross. What a strange symbol! The very instrument of torture of the God-Man. It is with this that his disciples are armed. They carry the cross throughout the world as a sign of their faith, like a burning flame that spreads from one place to another. Can you imagine a dead person being able to make such conquests; who has soldiers without pay, without hope of reward in this world, who is yet able to inspire them with the desire to persevere and suffer all kinds of privations?"

Napoleon was impressed by the conquests of Christ in this world—the army of bishops, priests, monks, nuns, lay men, women, and children, whose life is one of total dedication to him. Christ's Mystical Body, numbering today almost half a billion souls gathered under the world-embracing arms of his cross, does reflect, as in an imperfect mirror, the extent of his conquests of the minds and hearts of men. But his conquest is essentially a spiritual one, and it can be gauged only from the vantage point of eternity. It is *eternal victory* through the cross that Christ holds out to his followers when he says: "I will permit him who overcomes to sit with me upon my throne; as I also have overcome and have sat with my Father on his throne."

The final triumph for him who conquered through the cross, and for those whom he will have saved through it, is portrayed figuratively in the Apocalypse, where the court of heaven is represented as uniting in an exultant hymn to Christ: " 'Worthy art thou to take the scroll and to open its seals, for thou wast slain and by thy blood didst ransom men for God from every tribe and tongue and people and nation, and hast made them a kingdom and priests to our God, and they shall reign on earth.' Then I looked, and I heard around the throne and the living creatures and the elders the voice of many angels, numbering myriads of myriads and thousands of thousands, saying with a loud voice, 'Worthy is the Lamb who was slain, to receive power and wealth and wisdom and might and honor and glory and blessing!' " (Rev. 5:9–12).

17

His Cross And Its Exaltation

Those who have received so much through the cross should feel especially obliged to exalt it. Ever since the Son of God offered his life on the cross, the Church which he established has been tracing the sign of the cross everywhere. A century after the converted Pharisee Paul wrote "God forbid that I should glory save in the cross of our Lord Jesus Christ," Tertullian was writing that "we Christians wear out our foreheads with the sign of the cross." In the same century, St. Irenaeus was proclaiming that "Christ, by dying, has traced the cross on all things."

Two centuries later, St. John Chrysostom was to declare that "kings, removing their diadems, take up the cross, symbol of their Savior; on the purple, the cross; in their prayers, the cross; on their armor, the cross; on the holy table, the cross; throughout the universe, the cross. The cross shines brighter than the sun."

No days in the Church's liturgical cycle are more filled with dramatic eloquence than those on which she exalts the instrument of our redemption. In the triumphant unveiling of the cross in the liturgy of Good Friday, the Church has the celebrant exclaim three times, in successively higher tones: "Behold the wood of the cross, on which hung the Savior of the world!" All present kneel in adoration, as the choir each time responds: "Come, let us adore!"

It would be difficult to surpass the tone of exaltation conveyed in an antiphon used at vespers on what used to be called Holy Rood Day, the Feast of the Exaltation of the Holy Cross: "Hail, O cross, brighter than all the stars, thy name is honorable upon the earth. To the eyes of men thou art exceedingly lovely. Holy art thou among all things that are earthly. Thou alone wast worthy to bear the ransom of the world. Sweetest wood and sweetest iron, sweetest weight is hung on thee."

The Church continues to exalt the cross and to impress it upon all things. Non-Catholics might even suppose that we are forever erecting churches, monasteries, convents, schools, and hospitals simply because we want to surmount these structures with the cross. The Church, however, places the cross over buildings to signify the way in which she has first placed it in the minds and hearts of those who use them.

This exaltation of the cross is all the more impressive when one considers the playing down of the cross by those who have broken away from the Church. Those outside the Church who call themselves Christians more often than not appear shy and embarrassed in the presence of the cross. This certainly is not true of all non-Catholics. Cardinal Newman wrote one of the most profound sermons on the cross while still an Anglican. And *An Anthology of the Cross,* compiled by a non-Catholic, would surely be a credit to any Catholic. All that we are saying is that the farther one gets from the spirit of the Church, the farther one gets from the cross.

The Church has nurtured such a love of the cross in her members that they instinctively recoil, for example, from a church building whose dome or steeple is not surmounted by the cross. It is rather obvious that, while the Catholic instinct is to crown religious structures with the cross, most non-Catholics hesitate to do so, ironically preferring such a symbol of uncertainty as the weathervane. Non-Catholic artists often show the quandary of those outside the Church regarding the cross when they paint a church scene. A good example is a rather common motif showing a stately white church with a graceful spire. Usually you cannot see how the spire ends because the artist has decided to cut off its top with the upper border of the picture.

Perhaps there are artistic grounds for this device, although they are not apparent to the ordinary observer. A more plausible explanation is that they are the result of the quandary referred to above. Should the artist top the spire with the cross, or should he bring it to a point which will make it rather pointless and, therefore,

acceptable to those who like their Christianity on the vague side?
Not wishing to offend either those who are repelled by a church
edifice which is not dominated by the great symbol of
Christianity, or those who shy away from the cross, the artist ends
up with something which is both crossless and pointless. Maybe he
realizes that if he were to put a point on his spire, he would be
missing the main point, which is the cross.

So insistent is the Church on exalting the mystery of the
Crucifixion of the Son of God that at times she specifies that not
just the cross, but the crucifix, be presented to the view of the
faithful. She commands that there be the crucifix, and not merely
the plain cross, over the altar during the reenactment of the mystery of the cross in the Mass. It is the crucifix, rather than the bare
cross, that she presses to the lips of the dying. It is the crucifix, and
not just the cross, that she attaches to our rosaries. In this way, she
shows that, in exalting the cross, what is being glorified is not so
much the symbol as the reality. Even when it comes to the crucifix, the Church is concerned lest it be presented in such a way that
the full meaning of it will be blunted. Thus, in the encyclical
Mediator Dei, Pope Pius XII said that "one would be straying from
the straight path . . . were he to order the crucifix so designed that
the divine Redeemer's body shows no trace of his cruel
sufferings."

The progressively greater exaltation of the cross after so many
centuries is evidence both of the authenticity of the doctrine of
the cross, and of the Church which has exalted it. If the doctrine
of the cross had come from man, it would be exalted today, if at all,
only by some small sect of obscurantists.

When members of the Jewish Sanhedrin were of a mind to slay
the Apostles after they had started preaching salvation through the
acceptance of the crucified Christ, a Pharisee named Gamaliel
stood up and warned against any hasty opposition to the doctrine
of the Apostles. Today we are witnesses of the profound truth of
the words he addressed to his colleagues: "So now I say to you,
keep away from these men and let them alone. For if this plan or
work is of men, it will be overthrown; but if it be of God, you will

not be able to overthrow it. Else perhaps you may find yourselves fighting against God." It is almost two thousand years since the early master of St. Paul uttered these wise words, certainly a sufficient period of time to test any doctrine.

The Church could hardly do otherwise than to exalt the instrument of the world's redemption since God himself has exalted it. St. Thomas Aquinas writes: "Christ, as man, is the book in which are written all things pertaining to salvation. In the head of the book, in God's ordination, is written the Incarnation and the Passion."

Neither could the Church fail to exalt the pulpit from which the Word of God clarified and underscored the doctrine he had come to teach. As an unknown writer has expressed it: "The cross is the central point of the revelation of God to a fallen world. It has been compared to the Beatific Vision in heaven. Although in the cross we see through a glass darkly in comparison with those who see face to face, yet the cross viewed in relation to other sources of divine knowledge is the most luminous spot in this lower world."

The cross may be compared with the sun in the solar system, because all human destiny now revolves about the cross. By making the cross "shine brighter than the sun," we are making more certain that the doctrine which emanates from it will be unfolded, as Cardinal Newman said, "to the docile and obedient; to young children whom the world has not corrupted; to the sorrowful, who need comfort; to the sincere and earnest, who need a rule of life; to the innocent, who need warning; and to the established, who have earned the knowledge of it."

The Church has led countless hosts to glorify the cross. Among them have been intellectual geniuses and simple shepherds, statesmen and average citizens, artists and peasants, the literate and the illiterate. This testimony is the more impressive since the doctrine of the cross demands the humbling of the intellect and the sharpest curbing of the passions.

The exaltation of the cross is the fulfillment of the prophecy of him who conquered by the cross: "And as Moses lifted up the serpent in the desert, even so must the Son of Man be lifted up. . . . And I, if I be lifted up from the earth, will draw all things to myself." After quoting these words of our Redeemer, St. John adds, "Now he said this, signifying by what death he should die."

A columnist posed the question why Catholics, who make the sign of the cross at meals in their homes, omit it when dining publicly. The reason appears to be that most would regard crossing themselves publicly as flaunting their religion. If Catholics generally were to take up the practice, it would be regarded ultimately as a matter of course. Surely it would be unfortunate if any Catholic were to fail to sign himself through shame. He would thus be placing himself apart from the Church, for she is ever alert to find new opportunities to exalt the cross.

One who thinks and feels with the Church is forever seeking means for glorifying the cross. It can be worn on one's lapel. It can be placed on our doorposts, as Jews place on theirs the mezuzah, the scroll containing the Books of Moses. It can be displayed in automobiles. It can be floodlighted on church steeples. It can be placed in wayside or garden shrines. These are some of the almost countless ways of giving expression to the sentiment of the Good Friday liturgy: "We adore thee, O Christ, and we bless thee, because by thy holy cross thou hast redeemed the world!"

"The sign of the cross shall appear in the heavens when the Lord shall come in judgment," the Church proclaims in the Office of the Exaltation of the Holy Cross. She is forever preparing men for that day when he who conquered through the cross will come to judge mankind by its attitude toward the cross. Man's participation in that final exaltation will depend on how the divine wisdom and love which shine resplendently from the cross have been reflected in his earthly life.

18

His Cross And Our Lady

Because the Son of God chose to teach divine wisdom in a special manner through his holy cross, the cross throws light on every fundamental question that confronts us in this world. And because God always acts with munificence, the divine Master willed to have at his side on Calvary an associate teacher of wisdom.

This chapter is an analysis of Mary's contribution to the new and conclusive book of wisdom which the Incarnate Word of God wrote so masterfully on the cross. His Mother, by mirroring in her own person the wisdom that he taught, illustrates and illuminates each chapter.

1. HIS CROSS AND LIFE'S PURPOSE. The essential fact about the cross is brought out by St. Paul when he says that Christ was obedient, even to death on a cross. Thus on Calvary, our divine Master was exemplifying the one teaching that summed up his whole doctrine—that the entire purpose of life on earth is to carry out God's will. Here Mary could not have better fulfilled her role as co-teacher.

If our Lady had a motto, it might well have been her words at the Annunciation: "Let it be to me according to your word" (Luke 1:38). While it cost Mary a great deal to accept God's will on many other occasions, what it cost her to say "Let it be to me according to your word" on that tragic Friday afternoon will be known only in eternity. By accepting grief "great as the sea," she united with her divine Son in giving mankind an example of bowing before the will of God when it could not have been more difficult.

2. HIS CROSS AND THE HEART OF GOD. Never could love surpass that of the Son of God. His love was not one which was manifested in mere words. A blood-drenched cross is witness to the height, and the depth, and the breadth of his love. Yet, Mary's love for mankind was so great that Pope Pius XII did not hesitate to link her love in as intimate a manner as possible with that of the Son of God. "By the will of God," he wrote, "the Most Blessed Virgin Mary was inseparably joined with Christ in accomplishing the work of man's redemption, so that salvation flows from the love of Jesus Christ and His sufferings, intimately united with the love and sorrows of his Mother."

Mary's love is the most perfect reflection of the love of the God-Man possible in a human being. So perfect is the union of these two Hearts that we now use the expression, the Sacred Hearts of Jesus and Mary. If one is deeply moved by the love of the Son, one cannot fail also to be moved by that of the Mother. One must respond with gratitude to the one as to the other. This is why the same Pontiff wrote: "It is, then, highly fitting that after due homage has been paid to the Most Sacred Heart of Jesus, Christian people who have obtained divine life from Christ through Mary manifest similar piety and the love of their grateful souls for the most loving Heart of our heavenly Mother."

3. HIS CROSS AND PRAYER. Christ gave his final lesson on the necessity and power of prayer on the cross. The means he used to obtain strength to suffer his ordeal was prayer to his heavenly Father. Mary had learned the wisdom of constant prayer from her divine Son during the years at Nazareth. Absorbing the wisdom of her supreme Teacher to the end, she imitated him by spending the awful hours on Calvary communing with the Father. As he continued to pray for strength to accept his physical Crucifixion, she never ceased to ask for strength to accept his will regarding her mental crucifixion.

Because his prayer was offered with sentiments of perfect acceptance of his Father's will, it was a prayer of infinite fruitfulness. And because her will was more perfectly united with God's than that of any other purely human being, her prayer also bore incalculable fruit. Thus, Mary joins her Son in teaching mankind not only that strength to surmount great trials must be sought first of all in prayer, but also that prayer which comes from a heart that is in harmony with the Heart of God has tremendous power.

4. HIS CROSS AND HUMAN PRIDE. The world's greatest lesson in humility was given by Christ on the cross when he endured public humiliation the like of which can hardly be imagined. It is evident that every humiliation inflicted on him was also a humiliation for his Mother. Mary's anguish was increased immeasurably by seeing her Son and God mocked and blasphemed on a felon's cross.

Thirty-odd years before, Mary had sung of God's putting down the proud and exalting the humble. On Calvary she reads men the lesson that there will be no exaltation for them unless, like her, they accept and imitate the humility taught and practiced by her crucified Son.

5. HIS CROSS AND MATERIAL GOODS. Standing under the living parchment of her Son's body, Mary saw written there the greatest lesson in detachment from earthly goods ever given to mankind. Not only did she see Christ allow himself to be divested of his garments, but she witnessed his even greater act of detachment in permitting death to strip him of the body which had been woven from her flesh.

Our Lady had learned detachment very early at Bethlehem when she could not even provide a house for his birth. But her detachment reached its perfection when death, in stripping him of the human body which he had taken from her, stripped her of his earthly presence. Thus, as his able co-teacher, Mary gives man a living commentary on the wisdom of detaching himself gradually from the things of this world in order to grow in attachment to the things of heaven.

6. HIS CROSS AND A SENSE OF SIN. Surely nothing could show more clearly than the Crucifixion of the Son of God the awful meaning of sin. Isaiah said without qualification that the Savior was "wounded for our transgressions, he was bruised for our iniquities" (Is. 53:15). If Christ "was made sin for us," in the daring words of St. Paul, next to him, Mary felt the terrible weight of it on her innocent Heart.

Under the cross especially, Mary experienced the dread sense of sin which in our own times she has communicated through her wonderful apparitions. In the messages accompanying her appearances, our Lady spoke of sin and its consequences as though she had just come down from witnessing the price that she and her Son had paid for its atonement on Calvary.

7. HIS CROSS AND COMBAT. The most heroic figure in history is that of the crucified Christ. And if one can single out a picture of great womanly courage, it is that of his Mother standing under his cross. St. John, in saying that Mary *stood* by the cross, gives us a portrait of our Lady bravely serving with her Son as a breaker of God's just anger.

Mary was prefigured by Judith, the valiant woman of the Old Testament who entered the camp of Holofernes and slew him to protect her fellow Jews. The Church addresses to our Lady words which were first addressed to Judith: "Thou hast not spared thy life by reason of the distress and tribulation of thy people, but hast prevented our ruin in the presence of our God." United with her heroic Son, Mary gives a shining example of the fortitude which must be practiced in the battle of life.

8. HIS CROSS AND HUMAN HOPE. Through his saving cross, Christ completely raised the hopes of humanity made desperate because of its burden of sin. It was Mary who not only gave mankind its Savior but who joined him in the work of our redemption. On Calvary, Son and Mother united to restore hope to an otherwise hopeless race.

By calling her in the *Salve Regina* "our life, our sweetness, and our hope," the Church gives due recognition to the part Mary plays in the hope we have of receiving God's grace in this life and the glory of heaven. The Church readily applies to Mary the words of Ecclesiastes: "I am the Mother of fair love . . . and of holy hope."

9. HIS CROSS AND PENANCE. Of all those present on Calvary, Mary saw most clearly that her divine Son was enduring the endless agony of his Passion in atonement for the sins of men. She learned in the most concrete way that sin can be atoned for through suffering voluntarily embraced.

No purely human being ever needed penance less than Mary, for she was free from all sin, actual as well as original. Yet, apart from Christ, nobody has done more to make reparation for the sins of mankind. With all the more reason, therefore, could she urge the world, as she did in her apparitions, to do penance.

10. HIS CROSS AND ACHIEVEMENT. The supreme achievement of Christ was the saving of the human race from eternal doom by means of his redeeming cross. As his cooperator par excellence in this tremendous work, his Mother shared in his achievement. So important and intimate was Mary's participation in the saving of mankind from eternal perdition that the Church has never hesitated to give her the title of Co-Redemptrix.

By uniting her unbounded sorrow on Calvary with the sacrificial suffering of her divine Son, our Lady was vividly illustrating the doctrine that the suffering of every member of the Mystical Body of Christ becomes precious when joined with his. She was expounding in practice the teaching St. Paul was to enunciate in saying that he made up for the Church in his own body those things which were lacking in the Passion of our Lord. Mary could not have taught more clearly than she did on Calvary that all the members of the Church not only can, but ought to share in the achievement of her Son by uniting their crosses with his.

11. HIS CROSS AND PEACE OF SOUL. Peace is the tranquility of order. Man can be sure that there is order in his life only if his will is in harmony with the will of God. This is perfect order, which means perfect peace. On the cross, the will of Christ was in perfect harmony with the will of his Father. The God of largesse again adds to the example given to us by his Son, that of his Mother. As Fr. Garrigou-Lagrange says, "One cross sufficed for Jesus and Mary." We find in this fact a symbol of the harmony that existed between Son and Mother during the Passion, and between these two Hearts and the Heart of God.

Mary was given the title Queen of Peace during World War I. The Church wanted to impress upon mankind that peace could be had only if men would eliminate disorder from their lives. The only way of doing this is to have a will perfectly in harmony with the will of God. The test, as Mary shows, comes through the cross. She will more readily obtain the peace which mankind desires if man strives for it through imitation of her attitude toward God's will on Calvary.

12. HIS CROSS AND HUMAN RELATIONS. By dying for humanity on the cross, Christ gave the world the classic exemplification of his doctrine of love, for greater love than this no one has than to lay down his life for his friends. Taking her cue from the divine Teacher, Mary also taught love of mankind through the telling method of demonstration. Although she did not die for others, what she endured while standing under the cross was enough to have caused her death. "Happy the senses of the Blessed Virgin Mary," says the Church, "which, without dying, earned the palm of martyrdom beneath the cross of our Lord."

The Hearts of our Savior and his Mother were united on Calvary in sacrificial love for mankind. "The divine blood and the tears of the Mother flow together," writes Dom Guéranger, "and are mixed for the redemption of the human race." As was true of the sacrifice of her Son, all her suffering was for others, for she needed to offer none for herself. Under the cross, Mary gave an example of love for others only second to that of the divine Redeemer himself.

13. HIS CROSS AND LENGTH OF LIFE. By dying on the cross at the age of thirty-three, Christ teaches man that the important matter is not how long he lives, but the way he spends the time which God gives him, whether that time be long or short. By accepting the prolongation of her life into her sixties, Mary teaches mankind the same lesson.

By offering his life on the cross in his thirties, Christ is showing those who die early in life that they are not being cheated. He is teaching that, with God, quality is far more important than quantity, that a few well-spent years are much better than many years ill spent. Our Lady is teaching a similar wisdom. She is showing those who live to a more advanced age that long years, instead of being regarded as protracted waste, should be used to grow in wisdom and grace.

14. HIS CROSS AND ITS ANTICIPATION. Anticipation can heighten either joy or sorrow. Our Lord's knowledge that he had come into the world to give his life in the most brutal form of execution ever devised made his Passion as long as his earthly life. Mary also had to endure this torment by anticipation because as early as the Presentation of the divine Child in the Temple, she was told by a prophet that her own soul would be pierced by a sword.

It is likely that our Lady had to live with only the haziest concept of what form that sword would take. This perhaps was a merciful dispensation. The awful sorrow that would be hers during the Passion could hardly have been borne in anticipation for the greater part of a lifetime. Whatever the extent of her knowledge concerning what awaited her, there was no getting away from that stark prophecy regarding the piercing of her soul. Our Lady joins our Lord in giving a lesson in endurance to those whose trial is drawn out over many months or years.

15. HIS CROSS AND VICTORY. Human nature shrinks from suffering. But nature accepts suffering more readily if something worthwhile is achieved through the endurance of pain. Mary was the first to see clearly the close association between cross and

crown. When Mary had been told in the Annunciation that of her
Son's kingdom "there will be no end" (Luke 1:33), she realized
obscurely that her participation in the Incarnation of the Son of
God would result in participation in his eternal kingship. When she
saw that this also meant participation in his cross, she was strength-
ened to accept the ordeal because it would be followed by never-
ending triumph.

She thus encourages man, during the agony of the contest, to
keep his eyes on the prize—participation in the victory of the Son
and the Mother. She has been given the title of Our Lady of
Victories appropriately, because in the spiritual order the final triumph must be preceded by a series of victories. If one keeps in
mind the connection between her Assumption and Coronation on
the one hand, and her participation in the cross on the other, one
will the more easily accept one's own share in the Passion. Thus
one will, in a little while, reach her side and share her eternal glory
in heaven.

16. HIS CROSS AND ITS EXALTATION. There are endless
ways of exalting the cross. Men exalt it by adorning buildings with
it, by placing it in wayside shrines, by wearing it on their persons,
by signing themselves with it. But all this physical exaltation of the
cross would be empty if it did not proceed from minds filled with
the wisdom of the cross, and hearts inspired by the spirit of the
cross. Mary exalted the cross by having it imprinted on her soul.
Our Lady's exaltation of the cross consisted in her uniting herself
completely with him who wrought the redemption of mankind
through the cross.

Our Lady was not in a position during her earthly life to exalt
the cross physically. While she made at Lourdes what must have
been the most graceful sign of the cross ever seen in this world, it
is not likely that she made this beautiful gesture while living on
earth. What other way was there for her to exalt the cross but
through her application of its teachings to her life? By living the
philosophy of the cross, our Lady shows there is no more acceptable way of exalting it than living its teachings.

We appreciate Mary's contribution to mankind's understanding of the cross better by trying to imagine what a difference there would be in the whole story of the Passion if she had died before it started. The picture would have been incomplete. She who had such an important role in the Incarnation would have been expected to have had an outstanding role in the redemption.

If men are grateful to the illuminators of medieval manuscripts for adding beauty and vividness to God's written word, how much more grateful should they be to Christ's Mother for thus illuminating the Book of the Cross.

19

Epilogue

There is always danger, when we consider intensively one mystery of the faith, that we will not keep it in context with the other mysteries of the Christian religion. If any member of the Church were to concentrate his gaze on the cross and Passion of our Lord, and hardly ever think of his triumphant rising from the dead, there would be a lack of balance in his very devotion to the sacred Passion.

We can be authentic members of the Mystical Body of Christ only if we "think with the Church." The mind and spirit of the Church are made clear in the liturgy. In the liturgy, the Church constantly associates the sufferings and death of Christ with his Resurrection.

That some members of the Church do not keep the Passion and the Resurrection in context is evident from their attitude toward Lent and the Easter season. We cannot but rejoice that a multitude of Catholics enter wholeheartedly into the spirit of Lent, attending Mass daily and performing acts of penance and charity. This is what the Church desires and urges us to do during Lent. She is, however, far from wanting us to make Good Friday the climax of this outpouring of devotion. The Easter liturgy, which begins with the Easter Vigil on Holy Saturday night and continues for the eight weeks following Easter, is the true climax of the Lenten liturgy. It should not escape our attention that Eastertide, the season of joy and fulfillment, is longer than Lent, the season of sorrow and penance.

In the preface of the Mass of Easter, which is the preface that is said during the forty days until the solemnity of our Lord's Ascension, the Church links the death of Christ with his

Resurrection. The preface reminds us that "He is the true Lamb who took away the sins of the world. *By dying he destroyed our death; by rising he restored our life.*" In the Creed recited during Mass, we have no sooner finished saying that "he was crucified under Pontius Pilate; he suffered, died, and was buried," than we are proclaiming that "on the third day he rose again."

If we do not keep our Lord's Resurrection in view, we are not going to keep the whole mystery of Christ in focus. St. Paul wrote to the Corinthians that they would be saved if they held fast to the Gospel, *"as I preached it to you."* He then went on to summarize it, as he had preached it to them: "For I delivered to you first of all, what I also received, that Christ died for our sins according to the Scriptures, and that he was buried, and that he rose again the third day, according to the Scriptures, and that he appeared to Cephas, and after that to the Eleven. Then he was seen by more than five hundred brethren at one time. . . . And last of all . . . he was seen by me." The Apostle could not have made it clearer that those to whom he had preached could not be saved unless they understood and accepted Christ as crucified, and as risen from the dead.

The Passion of Christ, without his Resurrection, would have availed us nothing. St. Paul makes this evident when he says: "And if Christ is not risen, vain is your faith, for you are still in your sins." Nothing could show better than these words how important for our understanding of the faith, and our spiritual progress, is the association in our thinking of our Lord's death and resurrection.

All this is paramount for our growth in the virtue of hope, a virtue which, along with faith and love, is necessary for salvation. The foundation of our hope is expressed in the words of the Creed: "We look for the resurrection of the dead, and the life of the world to come." But our resurrection flows from that of our Lord, as St. Paul indicates when he says: "But as it is, Christ has risen from the dead, the firstfruits of those who have fallen asleep." He elaborates on this in writing to the Romans: "But if the Spirit of him who raised Jesus from the dead dwells in you, then he who raised Jesus Christ from the dead will also bring to life your mortal bodies because of his Spirit who dwells in you."

If our hope is not broad enough to encompass our rising from the dead at the Second Coming of Christ, it is a stunted hope, which means it is not hope at all. "If with this life only in view," says St. Paul, "we have had hope in Christ, we are of all men the most to be pitied."

While we gratefully repeat through the year the words which the Church places on our lips on Good Friday—"We adore thee, O Christ, and we bless thee, because by thy holy cross thou hast redeemed the world"—let us also remember the words of the Mass and Office of Easter—"This is the day which the Lord has made; let us rejoice and be glad in it" (Ps. 118:24).

This attitude toward the Passion and Resurrection of our Lord is not only necessary for the proper development of the virtue of hope, it is also necessary if we are to grow in that joy which is one of the fruits of the presence of the Holy Spirit in our souls. We do not love the cross for its own sake. We embrace it because of the joy that follows our ready acceptance of it. In this we are only imitating our divine Master, "who for the joy set before him, *endured* the cross." The psalmist was inspired to sing: "They who sow in tears, shall reap in joy." No matter how the thought is expressed, in these words of the psalmist, or as we express it, "Through the cross to the crown," let us bear in mind that Easter could not have been much closer to Good Friday, and that, if we share the cross with him, we will reign with him in eternal peace and glory.